STRESS-FREE VEGETABLE GARDENING

ISBN 13: 978-1-4621-1341-5

PUBLISHED BY HOBBLE CREEK PRESS, AN IMPRINT OF CEDAR FORT, INC.
2373 W. 700 S., SPRINGVILLE, UT 84663
DISTRIBUTED BY CEDAR FORT, INC., WWW.CEDARFORT.COM

LIBRARY OF CONGRESS CATALOGING-IN-PUBLICATION DATA

WARNOCK, CALEB (CALEB J.), 1973- AUTHOR.
STRESS-FREE VEGETABLE GARDENING : THRIVING GARDENS WITH MINIMAL EFFORT / CALEB WARNOCK.
PAGES CM
ISBN 978-1-4621-1341-5
1. VEGETABLE GARDENING. I. TITLE.
SB320.9.W37 2015
635--DC23
2015029857

COVER DESIGN BY LAUREN ERROR
PAGE DESIGN BY KRYSTAL WARES
COVER DESIGN © 2016 BY LYLE MORTIMER
EDITED BY EILEEN LEAVITT

PRINTED IN CHINA

10 9 8 7 6 5 4 3 2 1

PRINTED ON ACID-FREE PAPER

STRESS-FREE VEGETABLE GARDENING

thriving gardens with minimal effort

CALEB WARNOCK

author of The Forgotten Skills series

HOBBLE CREEK PRESS

an imprint of Cedar Fort, Inc. | springville, ut

CONTENTS

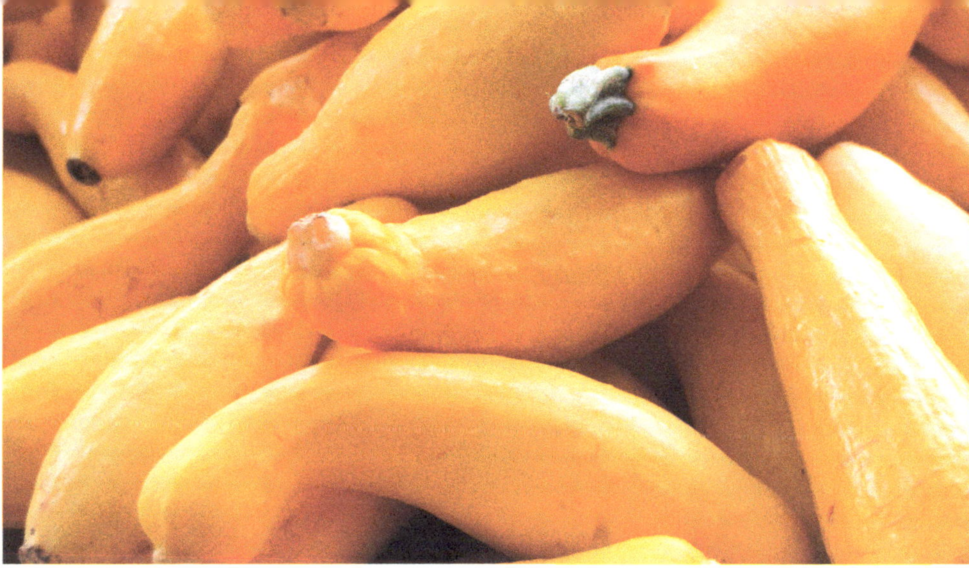

SEEDS WITH THIS SYMBOL NEXT TO THEM CAN BE PURCHASED ON CALEB WARNOCK'S WEBSITE: SEEDRENAISSANCE.COM

The Goal

Authentic Health, Flavor & Confidence in Nature & Yourself

"In these days of wars and rumors of wars, haven't you ever dreamed of a place where there was peace and security, where living was not a struggle but a lasting delight?"

—Title card from the 1937 Frank Capra film, Lost Horizon

I am on a mission to change the way the world gardens. This is not just another book on gardening. The goal of this book is to give you a no-nonsense approach to gardening without spending much money or time, while harvesting a truly old-fashioned bounty of authentic health, flavor, and confidence in nature and yourself.

You will learn how to garden hand-in-hand with Mother Nature instead of fighting her every step of the way. She wants to do most of the work. A bountiful garden is much easier to achieve when we get out of her way—the way gardening used to be done when people depended on their gardens for food—when gardens were not a hobby, they were dinner.

You might wonder, who is this guy and what are his credentials? Does the world really need another gardening book? Surely this guy has no new information, nothing to offer that isn't already out there. And how exactly does he propose to make gardening "stress-free"?

Here is the answer: Today, as I write this, it is March 27, 2015. We live on the bench of the Rocky Mountains at 5,200 feet elevation. My average frost-free growing season is ninety-two days and is still two months away.

Yet here is an inventory of what we have in our garden today:

- America spinach the size of my hand
- garlic (red and white)
- carrots (color mix)
- parsnips

In addition, you'll find the following self-seeded varieties (meaning I did nothing to grow it; it plants and grows itself and has not been watered or cultivated by me this year). These self-seeders need no care in autumn, winter, or spring but need water in the summer:

- fettle greens the size of my forearm, and rapini of fettle (kind of like broccoli)
- Dwarf Blue Siberian Kale almost a foot long
- Collard Vates (the size of my head)
- lettuces: Winter Green Jewel Romaine, Caleb's Deep Winter, Marvel of Four Seasons, North Pole (with leaves larger than my hands)
- chicory
- Swiss chard (I could pick buckets of it)
- Osaka Purple Mustard greens
- Vernal Red Orach
- Broad Windsor Fava beans (six inches tall but not bearing beans yet)
- medicinal herbs: German chamomile and plaintain
- leeks (lots of them, ready to harvest!)
- culinary herbs: parsley and cilantro
- edible wild greens: wild spinach (lambsquarters), common mallow, and shepherd's purse

Today's early spring garden also boasts a large variety of perennial plants. (These grow by themselves year after year and require no care in autumn, winter, or spring but need water in the summer.)

- onions (bulbs): Green Mountain Multiplier Huge, Egyptian Walking, Blanc Hatif de

Egyptian Walking Onion

Paris, and shallots in pink and yellow. These onions are three to four inches in diameter (except the shallots)

- perennial culinary herbs in large volumes: chives, green onions, garlic chives, lemon balm (melissa), thyme, and winter savory
- soapwort (leaves used to make homemade herbal soap)
- medicinal herbs: hyssop, horehound, eyebright, mullein, lemon balm, alfalfa, and dry lavender flowers still on the stems and highly fragrant!
- elephant garlic

All of these plants are outside, without protection, despite the freezing nights. This is a total of forty-four vegetables and herbs, and thirty-six of them are self planted or perennial—fully 82 percent of my garden at this moment!

In my geothermal greenhouse (which uses no artificial heat or electricity, and all water is harvested from the roof) on this day we have the following:

- Chinese cabbage michihili (ready to eat)
- Deep Winter lettuce (eight inches tall)
- Winter Green Jewel Romaine (eight inches tall)
- Swiss chard (fourteen inches tall)
- Cascadia peas with full, ripe pods of fresh peas
- turnips (Purple Top White Globe—several dozen bulbs ready to eat)
- Green Mountain Huge Multiplier onions (juvenile)
- Mountain Rose potatoes (These are probably not ready to harvest yet. I usually harvest them from the greenhouse in May.)
- Brigham tea (juvenile)
- carrots (Caleb's color mix, ready to harvest)
- fettle greens (the size of my hand)
- Vernal Red Orach (twenty-four inches tall)
- America spinach (ready to harvest)
- Chioggia beets (greens ready to eat but not the bulbs yet)
- common mallow

Also . . .

- stevia (in my kitchen in a pot, with leaves ready to harvest)
- nine laying hens in the backyard coop, giving us more eggs than we can eat!

In the garage (we have an actual root cellar but find our garage is more convenient) we have (and we use them almost daily):

- potatoes
- carrots
- onions
- parsnips

- turnips
- beets
- squash
- apples (from our trees)

My name is Caleb Warnock. I've written nine books so far on gardening and self-reliance. My first book, *Forgotten Skills of Self-Sufficiency*, unexpectedly hit the national bestseller list the third week after it was released. Today, just a few years later, the number of copies of my books in print is approaching one hundred thousand. I have given speeches, presentations, and classes to more than ten thousand people since that first book. More than two thousand people have toured our garden. I am the owner of an heirloom seed company: SeedRenaissance.com. I never expected to own a seed company, but after my first book explained my work to save some of the rarest and most important seeds in the world, people began to ask if they could buy my seeds. Today, my passion has turned into a full-fledged company.

I LITERALLY SEARCH THE GLOBE FOR THE LAST SEEDS OF IMPORTANT HISTORIC VARIETIES, LIKE WHITE PINEAPPLE-FLAVORED STRAWBERRIES, PERENNIAL WHEAT, PERENNIAL ONIONS, MEDICINAL HERBS, WINTER GROWING LETTUCES, AND SO MANY MORE.

I do a few important things that I believe no one else is doing.

I specialize in year-round, self-sufficient gardening for all climates. I literally search the globe for the last seeds of important historic varieties, like white pineapple-flavored strawberries, perennial wheat, perennial onions, medicinal herbs, winter-growing lettuces, and so many more. I am single-handedly keeping alive many critical heirloom varieties. In some cases, I am the only commercial grower in the world of these important seeds. I am trying to spread them around and save them from extinction.

For every common heirloom vegetable I offer, I've grown, tested, and rejected thirty to forty other varieties. I spend huge amounts of time and money on these tests, because no one else is doing this work. I evaluate how these varieties perform in an organic garden, without petro-chemical fertilizer, pesticides, or herbicides. I evaluate earliness, flavor, production, storage, cold-soil tolerance, winter harvestability, self-seeding capacity, and more. If I don't love a variety, I don't sell it. For example, I have grown more than six hundred heirloom tomato varieties (cultivars). I have grown every heirloom cantaloupe on earth. I have tested more than two hundred and fifty varieties (cultivars) of beans, several hundred lettuces, dozens of onions, and more than one hundred varieties of peas. I could go on.

Finally, every seed I sell is guaranteed

pure—never hybrid, GMO, patented, or corporate owned. I am passionate that our food supply *must* remain in the public domain. I am inviting everyone to join me in creating a renaissance in our backyard gardens. There is a better, easier, healthier, truly sustainable, stress-reducing way to garden, and this book will show you how.

My backyard garden

The Broken Law of Abundance in the Modern Garden—and Three Solutions

Okay, reader, let's take a deep breath together and be brave. This chapter might hurt your feelings. Think of it as tough love. I know this conversation makes people uncomfortable. Defining the problem is the first step toward change.

The Law of Abundance for the backyard garden is this: abundance must be available to everyone who chooses to participate.

As soon as abundance is only available to some and not others, the Law of Abundance has been broken. When the Law of Abundance is broken, the Law of Want prevails. Today, the Law of Abundance is broken, and because of it, there are wars, turmoil, and suffering.

Peace will prevail when the Law of Abundance is honored. The Law of Abundance will provide abundance for everyone, without victims, without lack, and without austerity. The Law of Want provides abundance for some and war and poverty for most.

Let me give a simple example:

Abundance: The people that planted, watered, and harvested my food had the same working conditions and wages that I would demand for my own children if they were doing that work.

Want: The working conditions of the people that grow my food are purposely kept secret from me because if I knew, I would be sick to my stomach. I would truly never want my children to work on farms anyway because that is a low-class job.

Food in the United States is mostly grown using the Law of Want. We can fix this. There is a simple solution. All that is required to make the solution a reality is public demand. The solution? Everything we need can be produced locally. In the United States, we don't grow our food locally because we don't want to pay a US wage for food. If growing food locally was profitable, people would do it. But making it profitable would mean it would cost more. And we don't want to pay more, so we go to the people in other countries, who are more desperate for work than we are. We can pay them less because of their desperation. So they do all the hard work, often in deplorable conditions. And we eat the fruits of their labors while they go home to desperation.

When we want abundance for all, we will produce our food locally and profitably. Think of it—being able to visit the place where your food is grown, to eat it fresh. No need for long-haul shipping, no hidden working conditions. Everything is out in the open, and everyone can see where the food is grown, how the food and people are treated, and how the land is treated.

FOOD IN THE UNITED STATES IS MOSTLY GROWN USING THE LAW OF WANT. WE CAN FIX THIS.

For things we cannot grow locally, we will pay the same fair price that allows the same lifestyle we live. If I want peace in the world, I allow abundance for all. I am willing to readjust my budget and lifestyle to make sure that I am not treating other people differently than I want my children to be treated (and paid). I might have to curtail some luxuries to make sure other people's children are treated the way I want my children to be treated. Candy, soda, sugary desserts, snack foods, fast food, and frozen prepared foods would be the best "luxuries" to start curtailing, for our own health, and especially for the health of the rising generation. More food, less junk.

This is really the ideal option.

The other choice is the choice we live today—a hidden economy where the desperately poor grow our food, make our clothes, and manufacture our "stuff" because we can offer them a pittance and they are in no position to decline.

The option I am suggesting (the option of abundance) used to be the way the world worked. By this, I mean for most of the history of the world, food was grown with true seeds (heirloom seeds) that were grown at home, using methods that required no chemicals or purchased fertilizers.

This can only happen if more people grow more of their own food in the backyard, depending less on mass-produced agriculture, which relies on chemicals, synthetics, machines, and impoverished labor. Every little bit of food we grow ourselves helps shift us back to a local economy that is self-reliant.

We as communities and counties and states can be self-reliant. Think about it.

If only it were that easy! some people have said to me on social media and in classes.

But it is easy, if we use our influence. We are in charge of what happens locally. We can support and encourage local growers, make better choices about our food, speak out about what we want, and ask our local grocery stores how many of their vegetables and fruits are locally grown—and if they are not choosing local growers, why not? We can support our local farmers markets.

I shared on social media a few sentences of what you have just read. What I had to say was uncomfortable for some people. You and I cannot change everything overnight.

We are responsible for our decisions. No one else.

We can change what we can influence. We can influence how our money is spent. We can vote with our dollars. We can break the cycle our nation is in. Breaking the cycle is not a global problem; it is a problem at home. Breaking the cycle is not a problem for world leaders; it is a problem for us. We are the ones participating in the cycle. When we change, the cycle changes.

Being tongue-in-cheek, some of my friends have called this attitude revolutionary—doing unto others as we would have done to ourselves. Exactly. That revolution begins at home. If we want a peaceful world for our children and grandchildren, *we must behave peaceably*. This means we cannot force others to do the work of harvesting and growing that we don't want to do, paying them wages we would not accept for ourselves.

Some people don't feel they are in a situation where they can grow food for themselves or buy locally. But they also don't want to buy food harvested by workers that are treated poorly. What can these people do? At the end of this chapter, I will spell out three solutions, showing exactly what we can do to influence change.

One of my friends told me they had watched a documentary about tomato pickers in Florida who were paid only one cent per pound picked. The workers went on a hunger strike, asking for a one penny raise, but the corporation that owned the farm refused. Raising awareness of these working conditions is the only way to create change.

There has been a lot of reporting in the United States about the plight of the people who work for us, growing our food. I hope each of you, my readers, will take a little time to find out more. When we know better, we do better.

By now, you are probably ready to wring my neck. Or you are overwhelmed and don't want to think about this anymore. Don't give up on me yet, reader!

This morning, as I write this, I was driving to an appointment when I saw a city employee wearing a white chemical hazmat protection suit, standing on the grassy strip that runs along the road. This employee was spraying weedkiller—almost certainly Roundup or the generic equivalent—to kill grass and weeds around the base of the city's trees.

This is a broad daylight example of magical thinking.

Let's walk through this logic together. Here is a chemical, which brand-new research, just published by the World Health Organization and the medical journal *Lancet Oncology*, says is "probably carcinogenic to humans" and may give people "lung cancer and non-Hodgkin's lymphoma."[1] A week after this new research is published, here is this employee wearing a hazmat suit. Someone, somewhere, recognized that this chemical was dangerous enough that the employee needed protection. But not dangerous enough to think, gee, maybe we shouldn't be using public money to spray this dangerous chemical on public land, into the air we all breathe, and into the local soil, mixing with the local drinking water.

This is the very definition of magical thinking. Somehow we know this chemical is dangerous enough that the person spraying it needs a full body protective suit—but spraying it into the environment must be just fine.

If you ask the experts why it is fine to spray the chemical, they will say "the solution to pollution is dilution." So while no one suggests it is safe to drink this chemical, spraying it everywhere is supposedly fine because it's just a little chemical liquid in a big world. Once in the ground, or in the water, or in the air, it will be diluted.

Every choice we make in our gardens and yards has real consequences. With every decision we make, we are either honoring or violating the Law of Abundance in the backyard garden.

In March 2015, the US Environmental Protection Agency released its annual report listing the companies releasing the largest amount of chemical waste into the environment, state by state. In Louisiana, the top polluter was the Monsanto chemical company, which released more than eighteen million pounds of chemicals into the land, water, and air. Though Monsanto released many chemicals, the largest percentage was formaldehyde, which the EPA classifies as a "carcinogenic chemical," which means it is known to cause cancer. This particular Monsanto factory is located in the "Cancer Belt" known for cancer clusters.

EVERY CHOICE WE MAKE IN OUR GARDENS AND YARDS HAS REAL CONSEQUENCES.

In case you are wondering, the instructions on an actual jug of Roundup say, "Avoid contact with eyes or clothing. . . . To protect the environment, do not allow to enter or run off into storm drains, drainage ditches, gutters, or surface waters."

I have been publicly maligned for my efforts to educate people about the risks of pesticides and herbicides. Some people, especially on social media, mistake me for having a "knee jerk reaction" against chemicals, technology, and progress in general. They assume I have done no research and that my concerns are facetious.

They are wrong.

Monsanto is a name known as a hiss and a byword among educated consumers who are concerned with health and clean soil. Number four on Louisiana's list of top polluters, however, is a name you might be less familiar with: CF Industries Nitrogen LLC—the largest producer of garden fertilizer in the United States. This company released eight million pounds of chemical waste into the land, water, and air in one year, according to the EPA report.[2]

This is our waste.

We might want to rail against and protest these two companies. But their waste is our waste. We cannot buy their product and then be angry at them because their manufacturing produced chemical waste. The moment we purchase one of their products, suddenly their chemical waste is our chemical waste. They made the product for us. If no one buys it, the factory will close, and the massive chemical pollution will stop.

We are the problem.

Over the past twenty-five years, the use of synthetic, petroleum-based fertilizers in the United States has skyrocketed. It has been many decades since the United States was able to produce enough synthetic fertilizer to meet our needs. Today, more than half of all the fertilizer we buy from the home improvement centers comes from the island nation of Trinidad and Tobago. Whether the fertilizer we spread on our lawn is made in Louisiana by CF Industries or made in Trinidad and Tobago by the Koch Nitrogen company, the pollution created by the factories is the same. Or at least we hope it is the same. While there are some standards in the United States, Trinidad and Tobago is reportedly lax when it comes to environmental regulations.

Both companies have several things in common. They use their local supply of natural gas to make nitrogen-rich ammonia, which is the main ingredient in synthetic fertilizer. Both companies pollute. Both are located near the ocean and are releasing chemical waste to the land, water, and air. Both are supplying US corporate farms and backyard gardens.

No matter who you are, this is your waste. If you eat anything made of corn or use fuel from corn, then you use the product made from this synthetic fertilizer. If you eat food produced anywhere on farms, it almost surely was grown with this synthetic fertilizer. If you eat out at a restaurant, you are eating food grown with synthetic fertilizer. If you eat meat or bread, you are eating synthetic fertilizer. That's right. Urea is a chemical manufactured from synthetic ammonia, which is used as a feed supplement for beef cattle. It is also the "food" that yeast companies use to grow yeast for selling in stores.

Where does our food come from? Well, the fertilizer comes from Trinidad and Tobago. And Russia and Ukraine. As I write this, Russia has invaded Ukraine because it wants to own their rich supply of natural gas. Ukraine is the second largest supplier of fertilizer to the United States. According to the United Nations High Commission for Refugees, more than one million people have been forced from their homes in the Donetsk region because of the new war over natural gas.

This is our war. We are a huge importer of Ukrainian fertilizer. Russia wants the huge cash generated from this business. We buy the fertilizer at the home improvement store, and the money filters back to Ukraine, resulting in one million homeless people because of the fight over access to natural gas reserves, and thus, synthetic fertilizer.

I know what you're thinking. This guy is

depressing. We are good people. We don't want to ask questions, because we don't want to be responsible for the answers. This is exactly how the people "in charge" of our system want us to be—just removed enough from responsibility that we don't foment change.

We want our food cheap, and we don't want to look too hard at how it is grown, fertilized, or harvested in order to keep it cheap. We don't want to know the long-term consequences. We just want the short-term low prices. Our logic? We deserve what we have.

The true problem with a broken Law of Abundance is this: there will never be peace as long as it is "us" (those who have abundance, which would be anyone living in the United States) and "them" (those who don't have abundance but provide the labor for our abundance). If you don't think everyone in the United States has access to abundance, travel to Egypt or Africa or South America, to name a few places, where you can see what real "want" looks like.

When laborers (who provide our food), and their children, become as important to us as our children and our lives, suddenly we see why the Law of Abundance is broken. Our abundance breaks their backs, so to speak.

Let me list some more examples of the Law of Abundance. Some of these are going to be harsh. Some might be hard to read. Some might offend you. Stick with me. I'm here to help. I am going to offer a feasible, real-world solution. Several solutions, actually. But first, examples . . .

Abundance: My vegetable plants produce true seed after their own kind.

Want: My hybrid and genetically modified seeds are self-suiciding, forcing me to buy seeds each year. The price of garden seed outpaces inflation.

Abundance: My garden is so healthy that pests and disease are naturally controlled.

Want: I'm plagued with pests, wilt, and disease.

Abundance: I grow the vegetables that thrive in my microclimate.

Want: I can get seeds from only a few big

nationwide companies. There is no one with a specialized, tried-and-tested knowledge of what grows best in my area.

Abundance: My soil is naturally fertile.

Want: The fertility of my soil depends on synthetic fertilizer and purchased soil enhancers.

Abundance: The majority of my garden is self-seeding.

Want: Every single vegetable requires lots of time and effort to grow, and who has the time or energy?

Abundance: The garden is designed for wise use of water.

Want: The garden doesn't grow unless huge volumes of water are available.

Abundance: My garden produces so much that I can give food away to those in need.

Want: My grocery bill burdens our family finances and causes tension in my marriage.

Abundance: We have fresh food from our garden 365 days a year.

Want: My garden is harvestable only in autumn.

Abundance: Everything my family needs is grown locally.

Want: Most of what we eat is shipped for hundreds or thousands of miles.

Abundance: We grow a bountiful garden without spending much money.

Want: The cost of gardening discourages me from growing food for my family.

Abundance: I know where my food comes from, how it was grown, what chemicals were used if any, and how safe my food is. I can choose to buy food that matches my ethical criteria.

Want: The origin of my food is vague at best, and the growers keep it this way on purpose, almost like they don't want me to know. I'm not told much about my food, and I don't have options.

Abundance: Our backyard chickens are fed self-reliantly.

Want: Our backyard chickens cost a fortune, and we can't sustain them without spending lots of money.

Abundance: The bacon we eat was locally raised on a farm we can visit.

Want: The bacon we eat was farmed in Mexico because the farm produces so much pollution that it would be illegal in the United States. But it's okay because the people in Mexico are okay with the way they live compared to the way I live—and if they are not okay with it, they should do something about it. It is their problem.

Abundance: My garden needs almost no fertilizer, and what little fertilizer I use is homemade from vegetable-based ingredients from my own property.

Want: The fertilizer I use causes war and pollution in places I have never visited, affecting people I don't know. It is destroying the health of lakes and oceans locally.

Abundance: We work in the yard and garden as a family. We teach the kids about health and self-reliance by example.

Want: We watch a lot of television and play a lot of video games. We spend much more of our free time inside than outside. The health of the kids is the responsibility of the doctor. We show our kids, by example, how to live off credit cards. We don't talk about our weight or health.

THREE SOLUTIONS FOR RESTORING THE LAW OF ABUNDANCE

1 **Grow more food for ourselves.**

This gives us control. It also gives us an appreciation for what it takes to grow real food. Most important, it demonstrates our values to our children and grandchildren. The entire purpose of this book is to make this solution easier for you.

2 **Guarantee that more food is locally grown by buying local food.**

When there is demand for locally grown food, more people make it their job. We already do some things to ensure abundance. All milk and most crops in the United States are subsidized using our federal tax dollars. The subsidy is a federal insurance program that allows farmers to stay in business when prices go too low. This is a good thing because it helps prevent famine and shortages. For example, the price a farmer can get for milk fluctuates for various market reasons. If the prices go too low, the dairy farm goes bankrupt. If too many dairy farms go bankrupt, there will not be enough milk to supply the nation. You can't open a new "milk factory" overnight. If too many dairies go out of business, it could take years to ramp up supply again. Milk prices could soar. So we, as a nation, choose to provide a subsidy, in the form of low-cost federal insurance, so that if the price of milk plunges temporarily, the dairy farm will get an insurance payment. That money will keep them in business until times get better. For us, the public, it means an uninterrupted supply of milk that is reasonably affordable. No one in the United States wakes up in the morning worrying that there will be a shortage of milk. Not everyone agrees with the subsidy, and it has been changed from time to time. The price of milk at the grocery store might be high sometimes, but there is always milk.

This is an example of how we have used our collective money (taxes) to create abundance. Almost all large farms get a similar subsidy for whatever they grow. We pay these subsidies to guarantee the food supply for ourselves.

Why not extend a similar type of subsidy to "micro-growers?" Our national economy depends on small businesses, but for some reason, we have given up our food supply to huge agricultural corporations. I am suggesting that we provide some kind of financial assistance or subsidized insurance and encouragement to jump-start the small farms of America. And I really mean small farms—a few acres or less. This would allow us to truly bring back local farms. Almost all of America has local dairy farms, thanks to the farm subsidy. Wherever you live, it is likely that your milk is being produced in your state. Even Alaska has dairy farms. We have local milk because of the milk subsidy insurance program. Why not create a similar program for small local farms, whether they want to produce eggs, lettuce, wheat, or herbs?

Such a plan would create many benefits:

- Our national food security would be improved. In the event of a global catastrophe, there would be local food.
- Local growers would know what grows best in their microclimates.
- Food would be fresher.
- There would be local knowledge of food production. School children, clubs, and groups of any kind could visit the farm and learn about their local food. For farms specializing in winter greenhouse growing in cold climates, visitors would surely come! This might, in a small way, encourage people better.
- We would be supporting our local economies instead of shipping food in from around the world.

OUR NATIONAL ECONOMY DEPENDS ON SMALL BUSINESSES, BUT FOR SOME REASON WE HAVE GIVEN UP OUR FOOD SUPPLY TO HUGE AGRICULTURAL CORPORATIONS.

I would also propose that there could be special programs for winter growing in cold climates, to help set up sustainable winter gardening of the kind that used to feed nations. There should be small farmer classes covering everything from organic growing to writing business plans for small farms. There could be regional small farm tool lending "libraries" including small tractors and other expensive equipment. We subsidize the price of sugar in the United States—why not look again at our priorities and what we really need?

There are ice-cream trucks that wander down the streets where I live, with their pleasant music alerting all the neighborhood children that sugar is just outside! Why not a local, cooperative "Farmers Market Truck" that would do the same thing, offering fresh, local food? There could be a smart phone app letting people know when you would be in their area, what the day's prices and specials were. We could create more "Local Abundance Basket" programs, where people buy a basket of local fresh food for a set price, first come, first served. These could be sold at the local grocery store, with the store getting a cut of the price. There could be quick-cook demonstrations and samples. Perhaps one co-op grower would specialize in carrots, another in lettuce, and another in beans or peas. Peaches, apples, squash—it is all possible, in season and, when possible, in winter-growing naturally heated greenhouses.

It all comes down to what we want. We vote with our money. No matter what grocery store you go to, there is far more space given to soda, candy, and prepackaged meals than is given to fresh food. Grocery stores give space to what people want. If we choose to eat local and healthy, we can change everything. None of this proposal will work if people just walk past the fresh local food to head for the candy, soda, frozen meals, and fast food.

It all starts at home, at our dinner tables.

3 Demand a "Dinner Table Bill of Rights"

Right now, the people who supply our food have a bill of rights based on secrecy. Their rights include the following:

- They don't have to tell us how their workers were treated.
- They don't have to tell us how our meat animals were treated.
- They don't have to tell us what pesticides, herbicides, or other chemicals our food was exposed to.
- They don't have to tell us plainly if our food was irradiated.
- They don't have to tell us if the food was artificially ripened or stored.

If we are the ones putting their food into our bodies after buying it with our money, why do they have rights of secrecy? We are the ones who have to live with the consequences, whether directly (our health) or indirectly (our environment). As consumers of food, we deserve a Dinner Table Bill of Rights. Here is my suggestion for what those rights should be:

- We have the right know where, specifically, the food was grown.
- We have the right to know what chemicals were used, by name.
- We have the right to know if the food was treated with non-sprouting agents or irradiated.
- We have the right to know how far the food was shipped.
- We have the right to know whether any unnatural, human-influenced process was used to ripen the food.
- We have the right to know, in plain language, whether the food was subsidized with taxpayer dollars.
- We have the right to know the wage range of the people who did the work and their working conditions. We have the right to demand decent and fair working conditions for the people who plant, nurture, harvest, and ship our food, no matter what country they were working in.

As I said at the outset of this chapter, abundance must be available to everyone who chooses to participate. If people choose something else, that is a problem of education. But when people are not given an option, that is slavery.

magically knowing what to do. I have worked hard for this. I have followed the money. I have asked hard questions—why did people used to be able to garden self-reliantly but today we are told that we must spend, spend, spend to make a garden a reality? What has changed? Who changed it? Why? What motivates the people who work to convince us that we cannot garden without their chemicals and fertilizers? How did the people who came before me do it when "all-natural" was the only option?

We can find authentic health for ourselves and our soil if we change. This book is dedicated to showing you how.

THE BEST WAY TO START THIS CHANGE IS TO GROW SOMETHING FOR YOURSELF.

When we refuse to grow our own food locally, we are forcing other people—desperate people—to do work that we do not want to do ourselves. Desperation is almost always answered with war. Peace will prevail when the Law of Abundance is the law of our land. The Law of Abundance will provide abundance for everyone, without victims, without lack, and without austerity. But only if we choose true abundance—abundance for all, abundance without victims.

The best way to start this change is to grow something for yourself. If you grow nothing now, grow something—even an herb in a pot on a windowsill. Don't give yourself excuses. Don't say you can't because you "weren't born with a green thumb." One of my greatest irritations in the world is when people say to me, "You were born with a green thumb. I could never do what you do."

Wrong.

I have earned every bit of knowledge that I have about gardening. I was not born

NOTES

1. Alice G. Walton, "WHO Says Monsato Roundup Ingredient Is 'Probably Carcinogenic.' Are They Right?" *Forbes*, March 21, 2015, http://www.forbes.com/sites/alicegwalton/2015/03/21/monsanto-herbicide-dubbed-probably-carcinogenic-by-world-health-organization-are-they-right/.
2. EPA, "2013 TRI Factsheet: State—Louisiana," accessed October 6, 2015, http://iaspub.epa.gov/triexplorer/tri_factsheet.factsheet_forstate?pstate=LA&pyear=2013&pParent=TRI&pDataSet=TRIQ1.

9 Principles of Successful Stress-Free Gardening with Benign Neglect

When people tour my garden (tours are given only for classes), there is always one recurring question: Do you do all this yourself?

Yes, mostly I do. I have some help now and then, but mostly I do it myself. AND IT IS EASY.

Sorry to use all capitals, but it is true. People think I'm lying or pulling their leg. But I'm not. I don't spend a lot of time weeding because I don't have to. The garden is designed to discourage weeds. I only watered my garden four times last year—and I live in the desert, in one of the driest states in the nation (Utah). I don't have a lot of time. I have a company to run. (Last year I shipped 1,420 seed orders from around the world and filled and mailed every single one myself.) I have contractual obligations to write books (thankfully!), and I have classes to design and teach. I have a large family. I do most of the cooking. And I like to paint, draw, sit in my hammock, and play outdoors.

I'm busy.

My garden MUST (capitals again!) thrive on benign neglect. What does this mean? It means that the garden has to do most of the work for me—it must thrive with as little attention from me as possible. It must not cause me stress, because who needs stress? (We also believe the same thing about children and pets—help them be independent. Sometimes it even works!) How is this possible in a garden? With careful, thoughtful design, using raised beds.

These are the principles of benign neglect gardening. Let's take each of these one at a time.

1. You cannot spend more than a few hours a year weeding.
2. The garden must cost very little.
3. The garden must produce volumes of food—that you will actually eat.
4. The majority of the garden must be self-seeding.
5. The garden must be a no-till design.
6. You must to be able to go on vacation for a week or two without everything dying.
7. You cannot force your kids or grandkids to weed, lest they grow up hating the garden.
8. The garden must use as little water as possible.
9. The garden must produce food 365 days a year, especially in winter in freezing climates.

1 You cannot spend more than a few hours a year weeding.

The number one complaint about gardening is weeding. Weed problems are the top reason people give up gardening altogether and become, how shall I put this politely, dependent on the grocery store. It seems to me that anyone who spends much time in grocery stores—as important and useful as they are—eventually spends less time in the veggie and fruits aisle and more time in the aisles of soda, bakery sweets, and frozen, prepared foods. Health drains away and the bank account too. Don't get me wrong—we go to the grocery store. But we spend as little time and money there as possible and try to eat as self-reliantly from our garden as humanly possible.

I'm convinced we would all be happier, healthier, and wealthier if we spent more time in the garden. And by time, I mean harvesting and relaxing. I have a chair in my garden, and I sit out there on summer evenings, watching the sun sink away. It's the only time of day, in July and August, when the temperature is Hawaiian. I live for those sixty minutes. It's like meditation. I feel right with the world.

Forget weeding. Relax!

How? This is only possible through careful design, and the specific design will be fully explained in the next chapter. For now, three things: First, learn which weeds in your area are edible and useful, and use them. We use mallow (medicinal and culinary), dandelion, purslane, and wild spinach whenever they are available. I grow these "weeds" purposefully in my winter greenhouse. Twice I have actually run out of mallow to harvest! Our pet rabbit, Puck (from *A Midsummer Night's Dream*), is also fed self-reliantly. He loves a thick crown of dandelion greens! And he turns them all into lovely, useful fodder for the compost pit. Second, I created a recipe for edible, vegetable-based weedkiller (available at SeedRenaissance.com) and wherever there are weeds growing that we don't want, we use that to kill them off. Finally, I don't believe in wasting time on an immaculate garden. Sometimes my garden is immaculate, and sometimes it is not. Our garden feeds us all the time, and that is my primary concern. I'm not bothered if there are a few weeds, as long as they are not out of control.

2 The garden must cost very little.

In spring and summer, if you look in your mailbox, you will be inundated with ads for your local garden centers and home improvement stores. Those ads try hard to convince you that gardening is all about buying stuff. Here is a short list of nonsense-stuff they will press you to buy:

- seed-starting "mini greenhouses" and special seed-starting kits
- fancy garden boxes and decor
- pesticides
- herbicides
- fertilizer
- any other chemical or spray or "dust" they can think of
- soil enhancers
- watering systems and gadgets
- live plants (my local nursery even sells juvenile corn for transplanting! Ack! What's the world coming to?!)

They have special shoes for you, cutesy tools, bags of this, jugs of that, every chemical they can think of, row markers, matching decorative garden "theme" sets, not to mention one special fertilizer for beans, another for tomatoes, and another for potatoes.

By the time you leave, you're bankrupt.

In this book, you are going to learn how to do without all that nonsense. We are going to get back to gardening hand in hand with nature, instead of fighting her every step of the way.

WE ARE GOING TO GET BACK TO GARDENING HAND-IN-HAND WITH NATURE, INSTEAD OF FIGHTING HER EVERY STEP OF THE WAY.

As you read the part of this book that is a vegetable-by-vegetable guide, you will discover that there are not many vegetables that need fertilizer, if you have a no-till garden (more on that in a moment).

And there are some vegetables and herbs that simply need no fertilizer ever:

- Summer squash and zucchini. I think I have mentioned in another book that I was, no joke, an adult before I learned that summer squash was supposed to be small when you eat it, not the size of a baseball bat. It's supposed to be six inches long. That is when it has the best flavor and texture. But this is not how I grew up eating summer squash. Why? The blame lies squarely on the shoulders of fertilizer. Summer squashes grow rapidly. In the heat of summer, from the time the blossom closes until the fruit is six inches long is seven to ten days. You can practically watch them grow. If you don't pay attention, very quickly they will get too big. Fertilizer forces them to grow even faster than they already do, making the already small window of time when they are ideally sized for harvest even smaller. Squash tolerate all kinds of soil and thrive. If you ask me (thanks!), the time to fertilize summer squash is never. Plant your summer squash in the worst soil you have, and you'll have perfect squash.
- Winter squash, same thing. If you are trying to win a giant pumpkin contest, yes, use fertilizer. But giant pumpkins are not great eating. Keep winter squash (also called storage or keeper squash) longer in the garage or cellar when they are smaller. The flavor is sweeter and not woody and fibrous when they are smaller. For best results, don't fertilize! All you need is naturally healthy soil.
- Greens. I'm talking about lettuce, collards, chard, mizuna, komatsuna, fettle, spinach, orach—any kind of greens. Have you ever noticed that in the store they sell these heads of romaine lettuce that are about sixteen inches long, and when you get home, you have to cut off and discard almost the entire bottom half of the lettuce because it tastes fibrous, like straw? It is woody and odd tasting, and the texture is off. This nonsense is brought to you courtesy of over fertilizing. Greens don't need to be fertilized. Sure, sixteen inches of romaine looks impressive in the store—but we want food we can eat, not food we have to throw half of away.
- Brassicas. (Brassicas are the family of vegetables that includes broccoli, cauliflower, kale, Brussels sprouts, kohlrabi, collards, and so on.) What they really need is to be transplanted early. Most people transplant them way too late. Brassicas need to grow in cool weather. By the time the summer heat hits, they like to be about finished producing their harvest. This is especially true because by autumn, the aphids will set in. Aphids love brassicas. By the time aphid season arrives, its best to have your brassicas harvested and the leftovers cleared out of the garden and into the compost pit. The only way to make this happen is to get them transplanted into the ground as soon as the soil can be worked in spring, or planted from seed the moment the soil can be worked. In earliest spring, they

will likely need some protection—a cloche, cold frame, or row cover. I find my reusable cold frames are the easiest solution—you just grab them and set them over the seeds or transplants.

- In a no-till garden, with soil with a high content of organic matter, most shallow bulb root plants don't need fertilizer. This would include turnips, beets, radishes, onions, and rutabaga.
- Cucumbers too, in a no-till garden, with soil with a high content of organic matter, certainly don't need fertilizer. Cucumbers are supposed to be sweet, crisp, and delicious. This means picking them at their prime. Fertilizing them only encourages them to quickly grow past their prime, which is a waste of time.
- Peas and beans, in good soil, don't need fertilizer.
- Cabbages can crack open or get so big that they lose their sweet flavor when fertilized. If you have good soil and you follow the instructions for brassicas above, you will get perfect cabbages.
- Herbs of any kind don't need fertilizer in good soil. The single exception to this might be basil, which I will include in the next list.

Let's switch gears. Here is a list of vegetables that benefit from one single dose of homemade fertilizer, given either in their youth, or just when they begin to flower (I'll explain what I mean by "dose" in a moment):

Cantaloupe

- Melons and cantaloupes. This fertilizer should not be too strong, and most commercial fertilizer is too strong (because it is meant to be tilled into the soil in spring, not applied when the plants are already established). If you use fertilizer that is too strong, it will burn the roots of the plant and can even kill the plant. I suggest you use a compost tea or a dose of homemade fertilizer, both of which are perfect and free. I'll give you recipes for both in a moment. If you give a strong fertilizer to a melon plant when it flowers, it can actually stunt the growth of the melon. If you give fertilizer after the melon has begun to form, it can cause the melon to crack (and so can overwatering, which is the reason so many melons, cantaloupes, and tomatoes crack open. You are watering too much, people!)
- Carrots and parsnips. You will harvest a nicer root if you give them a dose of homemade fertilizer tea about halfway through the summer.

- Basil benefits from a single dose just when the first leaves of harvestable size appear.
- Wheat. I know, I know, you are thinking, *Is this guy nuts? Who grows wheat in their garden?* Well, I do. And wheat benefits from a single dose just when it goes to flower (which means when the grain head first emerges).
- In good soil, tomatoes and eggplants don't usually need fertilizer. Some people will think I'm looney for saying so, but let me point something out. Most often, if the tomato is not the size you think it should be, it is because you have planted the wrong variety (cultivar) and not because you don't have good soil or because you need to fertilize. If you plant a Snow Fairy, those are never, ever going to be giant tomatoes. German Queens, however, are always huge. So make sure you plant the correct plant for the kind of tomatoes you want to harvest. That said, you can get bigger Romas and Amish Pastes with fertilizer, and some sandwich tomatoes benefit from a dose of fertilizer. Cherry tomatoes tend to crack if fertilized, and even sometimes in good soil. Cherry tomatoes should be planted by the summer squash, in your worst soil. Be careful fertilizing tomatoes. The smaller varieties (like Snow Fairy, Brandywine, Clackamas Blueberry, and Stupice) are more likely to crack than grow larger. And even Romas and Amish Pastes will crack if over-fertilized. If you want to fertilize a tomato, and you have good soil, give one weak dose when the flowers appear on the plant.
- Peppers can have a single dose of fertilizer if you wish, but overfertilizing them can cause them to stretch or rip open. Better to just have good soil if you ask me. (If you don't have good soil, this book will tell you how to create raised beds to fix that problem.)

Here is a very short list of vegetables that benefit from two to three doses of homemade fertilizer:

- Corn. Corn is a highly domesticated plant, meaning it bears almost no resemblance to its wild ancestors. Any plant that is highly domesticated needs special attention to reach perfection. I call these "high-maintenance" plants because they are like high-maintenance people—they constantly demand attention. Corn benefits from three doses of fertilizer. One as soon as it sprouts. A second when it reaches two feet high. And a third when it tassels out.
- Potatoes. Another diva plant. Why? Because we like the roots to be much larger than they ever get in nature. So we have to boost them with fertilizer. One common problem with potatoes is that they prefer a higher acid soil, which also helps them be more disease-free. The best way to do this is to plant them on a layer of pine needles, no matter where you live. And fertilize them well. Potatoes love blood meal and bone meal, and this is the only time I buy fertilizer, if I remember. Most years, I don't remember, but when I do remember to sprinkle a little blood meal

and bone meal, they do better. Blood meal is dried blood. Bone meal is ground up bone. These two together are the perfect fertilizer. Crushed animal bones, by the way, used to be sold by the barrel for use in the garden as fertilizer. We should still do that today, because they decompose over three to four years, so you only have to apply them about every five years. But back to my point. Potatoes like to have a dose of homemade fertilizer tea after they emerge from the ground, when they flower (or if they don't flower, about three weeks after they emerge from the ground), and then again three weeks later. Or, if it is easier to remember, once when you plant them, and then a month later, and a third time one month later.

- Fodder beets. If you are one of the rare people growing mangels (fodder beets) for livestock feed, good for you! More people with livestock should do it. The whole point of mangels is to get them huge—like thirty pounds each. They benefit from a dose when the leaves are two to three inches tall, another a month later, and a third a month later. Mangels also like good deep rich soil, so you can rotate them through your potato, carrot, and parsnip beds.

Now, drumroll please, because I'm going to give you my two free recipes for perfect homemade fertilizer. (These two recipes can also be found in my *No-Till Gardening* book and appear here courtesy of Familius Publishing):

COMPOST TEA

Step 1. Fill any size of bucket one-third full with compost. This should be finished compost, meaning whatever it started out as has now all turned into rich black soil (or brown, in the case of mushroom compost). It should be cool to the touch, not hot. Hot compost is still breaking down. This compost can be of your own making or purchased.

Step 2. Fill the rest of the bucket with water. Leave this outside to sit in a sunny place for three sunny days. You are essentially making sun tea out of compost. If you don't have three sunny days, wait until you have a total of three sunny days, or one week, whichever comes first.

Step 3. Stir the compost tea, preferably with something disposable, like a stick. Get two more buckets roughly the same size as you are using for the tea. Pour one-third of the tea into each bucket. You now have three buckets, each one-third full with the ripe tea.

Step 4. Fill each of the buckets with water. This step is essential. Compost tea that is not diluted can be too "hot," which means it is too rich in nutrients, and it can damage your plants. By filling your buckets with water, you have just diluted the tea using a two-to-one ratio. One part compost tea, two parts water.

Step 5. Use the diluted tea to water your garden. You can pour it into a garden watering can, or you can do what I do: take the bucket and pour it over the plants I want to water. Just be careful that you don't get the tea on yourself, because the tea will stain clothes and shoes, and it does have an odor.

GREEN LEAF FERTILIZER TEA

Because compost is usually in short supply in my garden because I use so much of it, I use this recipe most often. The upside is that you don't have to use your homemade or purchased compost. The downside is that this recipe has a stronger odor than compost tea. If you have a small property with close neighbors that might be offended by a tiny stinkiness for a couple days, this might not be the recipe for you. You can use the compost tea recipe.

Step 1. Fill any size bucket one-third full of green leaves of any kind. These can be weeds from the garden, the outer leaves of vegetable plants (like the outer lettuce leaves you would probably not use anyway), vegetables (leaves and bulbs) that have been munched on by the chickens, the rabbit, a caterpillar, grasshoppers (What's that you say—this only happens in my garden?!), leaves from trees (fresh, not dried), and chemical-free grass clippings. If you are using weeds, do not include weeds that have seeds on them. Weeds in flower are fine. The roots are fine. Dirt on the roots is fine. You can use all the same kind of leaves or a mixture of any kind of leaves. You can break open the baseball bat zucchinis and add them in, or tomatoes that were touching the ground and have begun to rot—anything from the garden that is vegetative and alive.

Step 2. Fill the rest of the bucket with water. Leave this outside to sit in a sunny place for three sunny days. You are essentially making sun tea out of green leaves. If you don't have three sunny days, wait until you have a total of three sunny days, or one week, whichever comes first.

Step 3. When the tea is ripe, carefully pour the water out of the bucket into another bucket, leaving behind the spent greens. The spent greens, which have now discolored, can be buried in the compost pit or compost pile, or hot bed. If you don't bury them, they will smell for several days.

Step 4. Stir the leaf tea, preferably with something disposable, like a stick. Get two more buckets roughly the same size as what you are using for the tea. Pour one-third of the tea into each bucket. You now have three buckets, each one-third full with the ripe tea.

Step 5. Fill each of the buckets with water. This step is essential. Leaf tea that is not diluted can be too "hot," which means it is too rich in nutrients, and it can damage your plants. By filling your buckets with water, you have just diluted the tea using a two-to-one ratio. One part tea, two parts water. This makes it safe for your plants.

Step 6. Use the diluted tea to water your garden. You can pour it into a garden watering can, or you can do what I do: take the bucket and pour it over the plants I want to water. Just be careful that you don't get the tea on yourself, because the tea will stain clothes and shoes, and it does have a strong odor. Don't worry, the odor disappears in a day or two. But not from the bucket. Rinse out the bucket with the hose, preferably over lawn grass, which can benefit from the residual nutrients.

Question: How much is a "dose" of this homemade fertilizer?
Answer: Enough to really soak the soil—as much as you would water if you were watering the garden with a watering can. There is no need for a precise measurement. You simply give the plants a good drink.

Question: Can I use my lawn grass clippings?
Answer: It's up to you. Did you put chemicals on your lawn grass? If yes, do you want those chemicals in your garden? I don't think so.

Question: Can I spray the tea on as foliar fertilizer (fertilizer sprayed on the leaves of the plant to be absorbed through the leaves)?
Answer: Yes, if you spray it straight. If you put it into one of those garden hose attachments, it's going to be too diluted. (Remember, you already diluted it once.) And if you try to put it in undiluted, it will stink and it won't be diluted to the right ratio. Why bother, anyway? What is the point of using it as foliar spray? It's easier and faster to just water your plants with it.

Question: How soon after I use the fertilizer can I eat my vegetables?
Answer: Wash them, and then eat them.

Question: How soon do I need to use the tea?
Answer: It can sit for several weeks if you like. It might develop a harmless white mold on the top, which you can skim off with a stick and throw out. The smell will get stronger. Your neighbors might glare at you. Don't let the kids or the dog accidently tip it over onto them—they will stink, even after you wash them with soap.

Question: Can I bottle it up to save for later?
Answer: Must you? Well, if you must, then yes, you can. However, only store the diluted tea—never store the undiluted tea, because it might develop gases and explode out of your container. Never store in the sun or heat for the same reason. Your best bet is just to not store it, or if you want to store it, don't store it for very long or in any place where you will mind terribly if it leaks or explodes and stinks. Don't store in glass jars, because of that whole explosion thing I just mentioned. Don't blame me if it explodes or leaks. And don't complain to me either. You are on your own!

Question: Can I put a lid on the bucket in case it smells or cover the bucket in some other way?
Answer: No, especially not if you are making the Green Leaf Tea. A closed container is very likely to explode, kind of like making homemade root beer that is too happy. You might be able to cover the bucket to make compost tea, but I have never tried it with a lid, so you will be experimenting.

The third principle of benign neglect gardening—the garden must produce volumes of food you will actually eat. If it doesn't, what's the point? This is not a sweet, flippant book about hobby gardening for a few fresh tomatoes and bragging rights. This book is about eating! The garden works for us; we don't work for the garden.

There is one enormously, hugely, gigantically important question that every gardener must ask him- or herself each spring: What can I grow that we will actually eat?

Should you give space to kohlrabi, cauliflower, and eggplant? Or carrots and greens?

Here are the rules of designing a vegetable garden:

- The most important things get the most space.
- The least important things get the least space.
- Some space is reserved for trying new things.
- No space is wasted growing stuff you know you are not going to use.

There are some basics that should probably be in every garden and probably deserve the most space:

- carrots
- potatoes
- onions
- greens
- raspberries
- strawberries
- tomatoes
- your personal and family favorites

When it comes to food, greens are nice, but roots are sustenance. We need greens, and they are easy to grow in volumes. But to really put health on the dinner table without spending a fortune, we need root vegetables. If you are not sure how to make delicious meals that your family will actually eat using the produce from your garden, see my book *The 100 Percent Natural Foods Cookbook*. While carrots, potatoes, and onions are the most popular root vegetables, there are a few others that are useful and helpful. If you are not growing beets, it's because your family is not regularly eating them—and if you are not regularly eating them, it is because you are growing the wrong beets! Try the Sugar, Chioggia, and Golden beets recommended in this book, and you will discover a whole new world of beets that taste and look nothing like the red bloody beets you grew up with. Turnips, parsnips, rutabagas, and radishes also go well in many baked dishes—and again, if you don't like these, it is because you are growing the wrong kind. If you don't like the flavor, grow the turnips and other roots that don't have the traditional flavor! Take my word for it, there is a whole world of delicious root vegetables out there in flavors and colors you don't see

Parsnips

in the grocery store. That's the joy of having your own garden—you suddenly have choices beyond the few varieties offered in the stores!

4 **The majority of the garden must be self-seeding.**

About 60 percent of my summer garden is self-seeding, and 80 percent of my garden is self-seeding the rest of the year. Here are some tips for creating a self-seeding garden:

- You must plant heirloom seeds. Why? They are the only seeds that grow plants that produce true seeds. Hybrids and genetically modified seeds do not produce true seed. You can read much more about this in my first Forgotten Skills book. When planting self-seeding seeds, you plant once, and you get a harvest for the rest of your life.
- You must have a no-till garden. More on that in a moment.
- You must not eat all the plants. Some must be allowed to mature and go to seed. They will "throw" their seed to the ground without any help from you. In autumn or spring, those seeds will sprout. You don't need to plant them, mess with them, or do anything to them all at. They need no attention or special care for winter or any other time. The only time you need to worry about them is in summer. The plants will need to be watered with your regular garden.
- Harvest from this second generation of plants, and again do not eat them all. The plants will go on and on for the rest of your life, feeding you happily. You will begin to notice that they are slowly moving around your garden. They will move a few feet or more each year. Just let them move around. If they try to move "out of bounds," then transplant some of them. Otherwise, no worries, no work, just harvesting!

WHEN PLANTING SELF-SEEDING SEEDS, YOU PLANT ONCE, AND YOU GET A HARVEST FOR THE REST OF YOUR LIFE.

Some vegetable varieties are simply more willing to self-plant than others. Over the years, I've taken note of my best volunteers so I can recruit them year after year. After all, if there is a vegetable that wants to plant itself, I'm too busy to argue and only too grateful to have the help.

Be willing to share your pathways. Self-seeders often plant themselves in garden pathways. If they have planted enough of themselves in your regular garden beds, you could simply pull them out of your pathways. You can transplant them when they are young if they are in the way.

Last, you will need to prevent crossing. For lettuces, beans, and tomatoes, this is not really a problem for reasons that are outside the scope of this book, but Asian greens, for example, are notorious for promiscuous cross-pollination. If you have more than one variety flowering at a time, your self-seeding crossers will change over time and are likely to slowly die out.

Here is a list of the best self-planting vegetable varieties. All of these are available at my company, SeedRenaissance.com, which is the only company in the world that I know of testing vegetables for self-seeding reliability:

Buttercrunch Lettuce

This is a green, sweet, crisp loose-leaf lettuce that seems to love to self-seed. Just make sure you keep an eye on it in the spring so you don't mistake it for an early weed and pull it out! In my garden, this lettuce comes back year after year if grown on ground you don't till. It is not a true perennial, but it self-seeds extremely reliably if you let a few heads go to seed. This is dwarf sized, with green leaves. It grows fast and works well for fresh winter garden growing as well as summer.

Gabriella Lettuce

This lovely burgundy lettuce comes back with good reliability, and it is always startling to find it growing in my garden pathways and beds with its striking color. It has great flavor too. This lettuce is rare and almost impossible to find, and I am proud to offer it to other gardeners via my website.

Marvel of Four Seasons Lettuce

There is a reason this lettuce has been a garden favorite for more than five hundred years—yes, you read that right! With the correct conditions, this determined lettuce self-seeds like clockwork. It is a favorite of ours because of its stunning color—a red/bronze/green with touches of purple. (In cold weather, it is mostly purple). The lettuce also has a better taste than most lettuces—and best of all, it grows well during all four seasons, including in a cold frame in winter.

Extra Dwarf Pak Choi

This super-fast-growing little Chinese loose-leaf cabbage is succulent and in demand since being featured in my first book. It will self-seed in your garden in both spring and fall! I've actually had this Asian green go to flower in my garden on December 5! It's great for fresh eating or steaming.

Indian Woman Yellow Bush Bean

A self-seeding bean is unusual, so you can imagine how caught off guard I was when I discovered its self-perpetuating tendencies. It doesn't self-seed thickly, but it reliably produces at least as many new plants as the number of plants the seed came from, if not more, which is pretty staggering for a bean plant. This bean is also super early, and rare and hard to find. In fact, the last time I checked, my seed site was the only place to offer this seed for sale.

Vernal Red Orach

This beautiful vegetable is one of my all-time favorites. It is popular in Europe but little known here. I'm on a one-man crusade to popularize this vegetable in North America. Beyond all of its other virtues (color, taste, nutrition, cold-hardiness), it is one of the single best self-seeders I've ever encountered.

Osaka Purple Mustard Greens

This has a dark purple color—the colder it is, the more purple it is—and it is a prolific plant. The flavor is hot when it is eaten raw, and I've had some people compare the flavor to horseradish. The heat almost totally disappears when sautéed or steamed. This green stays fresh though January or longer in a cold frame. It works well for fresh winter garden growing as well as summer.

Noir des Carmes Cantaloupe

This is a remarkable melon for so many reasons, not the least of which is its uncanny ability to self-seed. In fact, it self-seeds in my garden every year. I've been studying this melon for several years, and there is mounting evidence that it is self-pollinating, which may contribute to its unusual tendency to self-seed. This is both a winter and summer cantaloupe, traditionally grown in hot beds starting in January. I have also sprouted this melon in the first week of February this year in my geothermal greenhouse. Of course it can also be sown directly in the garden for summer growing. This is my favorite melon, and it grows prolifically—tons of melons—without any black plastic. It's also one of the earliest melons. And best of all, it turns from dark green to orange overnight when it is ripe, so you never have to guess.

Purple Top Globe Turnip

Not many root vegetables are reliable self-seeders, but this turnip breaks the mold. If every vegetable self-seeded as reliably as this turnip, none of us would ever have to plant a garden again. It has a wonderful heirloom turnip taste, and is a hardy plant—great for using in roast vegetable dishes and soups. It has a beautiful purple ring around a white globe, with white flesh inside.

Mountain Rose Potatoes

I've fallen in love with this potato. It is extraordinarily early—so early I can grow two harvests a year, and three when I use the greenhouse, believe it or not. This year, we harvested our first Mountain Rose potatoes from the geothermal greenhouse on Mother's Day for eating—a staggering accomplishment that goes a long way for any house trying to be more self-sufficient. This potato is so cold-hardy and so vigorous that it self-seeds remarkably by simply accidentally leaving a potato in the ground—or in the straw beds, where I grow my potatoes. Unfortunately, these potatoes can be hard to find. I try to offer a group purchase each spring on SeedRenaissance.com if they are available.

Dwarf Siberian Blue Kale

I don't ever have to plant kale anymore because my dwarf Siberian blue takes care of itself. If you ask me, any vegetable that takes care of itself tastes twice as nice! This is a beautiful plant with perfect flavor. This is popular for green smoothies and is good as a salad ingredient or sautéed by itself as a side dish.

Caleb's Winter Fine Fettle Greens

These have been self-seeding in my garden for years now, and we make good use of them, putting them in stir-fry, yakisoba, salads, and green smoothies. This is a vegetable that I created specifically for growing over winter without any protection in freezing climates. Nothing could be simpler to grow. And our pet rabbit loves them too. We pick them for him.

America Spinach

This is the world's best winter spinach—and it's great in summer too! Spinach plants are entirely male or female, so you need to let at least ten plants go to seed to get good seeding. For a better crop, let twenty plants go to seed.

Broad Windsor Fava Beans

These beans flower in the snow. They are extraordinary and self-seed easily. If left on the plant, the pods turn black and fall to the ground—and in early spring, you will have bean plants, with bean pods harvestable in April (at my elevation, 5,200 feet. The lower your elevation, the earlier and longer your growing season will be. Mine is one of the latest—the shortest in the country.)

Collard Vates

I planted these once and they have been growing in my garden ever since. Like my Fettle Greens, they go in stir-fry, yakisoba, salads, and in green smoothies.

Egyptian Walking Onions

These are both perennial and self-seeding, though that is a bit of a misnomer because they don't produce seeds; they produce onion bulbs both at the roots and on top of the plant. The bulbs on the top drop to the ground in fall and plant themselves. If you plant them once, you will have them rest of your life.

Green Mountain Multiplier Huge Onions

These are the largest onions I have ever grown, and even the smallest bulbs were larger than the largest bulbs of all of the other onions I have grown—read that twice! I wouldn't be without them. These don't actually self-seed either. They multiply (also called potato onions), meaning one bulb divides into many. You harvest most of the cluster and leave one to overwinter and multiply the next year.

Shallot Onions

These are small French specialty onions with a delicate flavor. I have pink, purple, white, and yellow varieties and love them all. (The pink are very rare indeed, given to me by one of the last growers in the world). Like the Green Mountains, they multiply. One bulb divides into many—often two dozen.

Snow Fairy Tomatoes

Not only do these reliably self-seed, the self-seeded plants produce ripe tomatoes just before the transplants from my greenhouse! This is also the best tomato for harvests in a winter-growing greenhouse.

Culinary and Medicinal Herbs

Many of these are either self-seeding or perennial. These include the following:

- German chamomile (self seeding; calming herb for tea)
- medicinal catnep (perennial; I prefer the old-fashioned spelling; used to calm nerves and rowdy children)
- yarrow (perennial; flowers treat respiratory ailments)
- self-heal (perennial; wound healing and sore throats)
- mullein (self-seeding; used to make a homemade version of NyQuil)
- peppermint (perennial; used for headaches, homemade toothpaste, and more)
- spearmint (perennial; topical muscle relaxant)
- yucca (perennial; used to make herbal soap)
- soapwort (perennial; used to make herbal soap)
- eyebright (perennial; used for eye strain)
- plantain (self-seeding; promotes wound healing)
- Brigham tea (also called Mormon tea; perennial; natural source of ephedra for respiratory and energy)
- ma huang (perennial; another natural form of ephedra)
- horehound (perennial; used for sore throats)
- hyssop (perennial; used for respiratory ailments)
- echinacea (also called Purple Coneflower; perennial; boosts the immune system)
- licorice (perennial; boosts the immune system)
- motherwort (perennial; used for women's health)
- oregano (perennial; culinary and respiratory)
- thyme (perennial; culinary)
- parsley (self-seeding; boosts the immune system)

5 **The garden must be a no-till design.**

For full information on creating a no-till garden, see my book *No-Till Gardening for Absolute Beginners*. Meanwhile, here are some of the important concepts. Natural soil fertility comes when the soil is not moved. If you till (deeply cultivate), you destroy a complex natural balance and synergy going on below the ground. To thrive, plants must have both water-soluble nutrients (nutrients absorbed in water) and water-insoluble nutrients (nutrients that do not dissolve into water). Something called mycelium below the ground provides complete nutrition to plants. Mycelium is a living network. If you till, you destroy it. If you destroy it, you have no choice but to use laboratory formulated fertilizers that make water insoluble nutrients soluble in water so you don't need mycelium and you can "beat" Mother Nature at her game. Why bother? Let Mother Nature do her work. When you switch to a no-till garden, you have much less work to do, you don't have to purchase a tiller, you don't have to rattle your bones tilling (it makes you sore as heck!), you don't have to buy gasoline for your tiller, and your machine does not emit fumes because you are not running a machine. The best way to get started is to follow the instructions in the next chapter for designing a raised bed garden.

15 Reasons to never till your garden again! (Courtesy of SeedRenaissance.com)

1. Dramatically reduces the work required to garden
2. Reduces weeding by 90 percent
3. Allows you to establish a self-seeding garden
4. Means you never need to purchase fertilizer again
5. Hugely cuts down on soil disease
6. Prevents soil compaction
7. Dramatically increases natural soil fertility
8. Makes a 100 percent organic garden practical
9. Makes gardening physically accessible
10. Makes permaculture truly possible—no gas, no tiller
11. Makes a garden honestly sustainable
12. Makes gardening easier for beginners and experienced growers, the physically disabled, seniors, children, and families
13. Increases yields
14. Makes a larger garden possible with less work
15. Makes gardening less expensive

Step-by-step instructions for creating a no-till garden are beyond the scope of this book. In my book *No-Till Gardening for Absolute Beginners,* you will learn how to

- use no-till to reduce weeds by 90 percent
- create a self-seeding no-till garden
- never purchase fertilizer again
- use no-till for all-natural disease control
- make organic gardening practical and simple
- use three methods of no-till gardening (ground, raised, hugelkultur)
- create naturally healthy, fertile garden soil
- convert an existing garden to the no-till method

6 You must to be able to go on vacation for a week or two without everything dying.

This is a real consideration. Sometimes we need to leave town. Or we get sick or have a family emergency or have an unexpected project thrust upon us. If the garden cannot go on without you, you have a problem. If you have the kind of garden that must be watered constantly and requires constant tending, you'll probably give up gardening soon anyway—who has the time? In the benign neglect garden, the roots must have access to the native soil, which is almost always the perfect soil mix for your climate. When you design your raised beds correctly (as outlined in the next chapter), the roots will have access to Mother Nature's water reserves.

At first, many people simply find this too astonishing to believe. Remember, I live in a desert with intense triple-digit heat in July and August, and last year I watered my established garden four times. I'm pretty proud of that. Remember, when you work with Mother Nature and not against her, your life and garden are going to be simpler. But you still don't believe me—so here is a way you can prove it to yourself. As I write this, there has been no decent rain for more than a month. Yet my garden thrives. Why? Because there is water in the soil. To find it, wait until you have had a drought period for at least three weeks. Dig down four inches into your native soil—not your compost or your raised beds. Dig into your native soil. If the soil is moist (not wet, but moist) then you have water. Your plants will be fine. In fact, your plants are "digging in," extending their roots deeper into Mother Nature's water reserves.

My soil is sandy, you might say. Well, try the test above. If your soil is dry four inches down, then when you build your raised beds, put a layer of clay in the bottom of the raised beds. Use shallow beds, as described in the next chapter, and fill them half-full of clay medium, which you can buy at any gardening center.

7 You cannot force your kids or grandkids to weed, lest they grow up hating the garden.

This is a big deal to me. No—not because my parents forced me to weed the garden. In my childhood, it was the opposite. I begged them to plant a garden, and I loved it. Sometimes I was assigned to weed, and I grumbled and kvetched, I'm sure. I was a kid. But mostly in my youth, it was me pushing my parents to have a garden. When I was about ten, my grandfather gave me my first gardening book, on how to grow strawberries, and I created my first personal garden—and I had that strawberry raised bed on the side of the house until I moved away to college. I loved eating those strawberries! Later, as a teen, I had flower gardens and some vegetables, and my garden was my escape from the world—the one place where I felt peace, safety, and beauty. (Well, in my garden and at my grandparents' houses, and in the desert, where I would wander for fun, studying the plants. I'm starting to sound like a real nerd here!)

Anyway, back to my point. What the garden needs more than anything in the world is children. The way that people learn to love to garden is by spending time in a garden.

Don't make the garden a punishment for your children and grandchildren! Make it a place they long to be. Let them eat the fresh tomatoes; mow (with their mouths) through the pole beans; search for raspberries, strawberries, and blackberries; and pick the carrots (they love the surprise—what color will it be?

how long? what will we make with it today?). Let them learn to love the garden!

The same should be true for all of us. If you don't love your garden—if it is not your pleasure and your respite from the world, it will become your stress and just another problem, and soon you will find yourself with a weed patch and freezer full of frozen prepared foods. If this book doesn't save you and your family from that fate, I will have failed. (Don't worry about me. I will get up, dust off, and find a new way to be useful. It's my life motto.)

LET THEM LEARN TO LOVE THE GARDEN!

8 **The garden must use as little water as possible.**

You might be thinking, *Um, we already talked about this.* And we did, kind of. But in July and August, you will panic and start overwatering. Why?

The Panting Pepo.

There is one single reason that most people overwater their garden, and that is the pepo species of squash. About half of the pepo varieties—including summer squash and zucchinis, many orange pumpkins, and even a few non-pepos—use a unique cooling system when the temperature gets over ninety degrees or so. They pant. Kind of like a dog pants its tongue in the heat. Except a panting squash looks wilted. People see these wilted squash and they are sure their garden is dying, so they turn on the water.

The problem is, no matter how much you water, they will keep panting in the heat, and you will keep thinking they are dying.

Luckily, there is an easy way to discern between a happily panting pepo and a squash that is truly dying of thirst. Simply go out to your garden in the afternoon and observe which squash are wilted. Then, return at dusk, just before the sun sets. Panting pepos will have begun to visibly unwilt themselves in the last half-hour of daylight, as the temperature cools, even though they might not be totally unwilted by dark. (They will be totally unwilted when morning arrives.) Truly thirsty squash will still be wilted at sunset. If they are, then you know you need to water—and I recommend a heavy overnight watering, and then leave them alone for eight to ten days.

However, if your carrots look wilty, they need water. Carrots are a great barometer of garden soil water, because their roots are deep, and they are usually planted in the most friable (loose, loamy, fastest draining) soil in the garden. So if your carrot leaves look limp, it is time to water.

When you water, go deep and long. Water overnight. Why? The sun is not out to evaporate the prized moisture. (Where I live, with little humidity, the air sucks up water whenever it can.) Vegetables will grow deep, strong roots if they are watered deeply and then not watered again until they truly need it. If you put vegetables on a drip line, or water two to three times a week, you will waste a lot of water, and your plants will be basically hydroponic.

I want to make clear that when I say in

this book that I watered my garden four times last year, I am talking about my mature, established garden. I am not talking about watering seeds and transplants. Many seeds and transplants in my garden are planted in early spring, as soon as the ground can be worked. These include everything with cold soil tolerance, like carrots, beets, parsnips, turnips, brassicas, Asian greens, winter lettuces, onions, potatoes, radishes, perennials, and peas. Because these are planted so early in the season, I usually need to water them only on the day they are planted (as seed) or transplanted (as live plants coming outside from my greenhouse to my garden). If the year is dry, I may need to water one or two more times, but usually there is enough moisture in spring and less evaporation, so very little watering needs to happen. Once the full summer heat hits, these vegetables are either deeply rooted (carrots, turnips, and so on) or ready to harvest (greens, for example).

Some vegetables can be planted only in the full heat of summer, like corn, watermelons, beans, and basil. These are watered on a "Plus One" schedule, following this pattern: First day, plant and water. Second day, water again. Then skip a day of watering, water, skip two days, water, skip three days, water, and so on until you are going ten days between waterings. Then water deeply, preferably overnight so that the water soaks into the ground instead of evaporating in the sun.

If you need to be away from home for a week or two, and you, like me, don't have an automatic garden watering system, water deeply the night before you leave, no matter how recently you watered.

All that said, everyone has a different microclimate. If your watering system is working for you, and you are happy with the results, don't change what you are doing. Except if you see panting pepos. Don't let those devious little suckers fool you.

9 The garden must produce food 365 days a year, especially in winter in freezing climates.

I wrote a whole book about this. It's called *Backyard Winter Gardening: Vegetables Fresh and Simple, In Any Climate without Artificial Heat or Electricity the Way It's Been Done for 2,000 Years*. I recommend it. I know the author, and he is a genius. Pure genius.

Jokes aside, if you want to grow fresh food year-round, there is no other book like this one. One of the great joys of my life is that people have begun to send me photos of their winter gardens from all over. I love it!

Benign Neglect Gardening, Raised Easy

There are only two purposes for raised beds. The first is to control the soil quality. The second is to control the weeds. In my book *More Forgotten Skills,* I give extremely detailed information about how to design and construct a raised bed garden while spending almost nothing. Because some of this information is critical to success, I'm going repeat the highlights here.

Raised Beds to Control Soil Quality

The native clay soil where I live is magnificent at storing water during the scalding heat of summer—it is the ultimate water-wise soil. But it also has some significant drawbacks when it comes to gardening.

1. The soil is filled with weed seeds.
2. It is full of rocks—big and small.
3. My soil is naturally alkaline, as is most soil in the western United States. This can make it difficult to sprout some vegetable seeds.
4. In the heat of summer, the topsoil is as hard as rock.

To overcome the rock problem, you create a rock-free layer above the rocks. To raise the soil acidity level, you add a layer of compost. To avoid the hard soil that fights seed sprouting, you create a loamy raised layer. To let sleeping weeds lie, you create a barrier. A single raised gardening bed does all of this, and this chapter will tell you how to do it at little or no cost.

Raised Beds to Control Weeds

You can't escape weeds. You can only awaken them.

Weeds are no fools. You can spray them, till them, solarize them, cover them, pull them, cut them—but as soon as there is water and light, new weeds will sprout. They have been designed by nature to vigorously defend themselves against the threat of eradication or extinction. The best way to control weeds is not to awaken the seeds—instead, let weed seeds sleep under a nice raised bed "blanket." This is what a raised bed does; it lets sleeping seeds keep sleeping.

Basic "Recipe" for Building Raised Beds

Here is the basic recipe, which is explained in detail below:

1. Build a frame.
2. Line the ground inside the frame.
3. Fill the frame.
4. Put a "topping" on the filler.
5. Plant your seeds and garden!

How Long? How Wide?

I strongly suggest you don't build raised boxes wider than the reach of your arm. The wider they are, the harder they are to plant, harvest, and weed (even if weeding is drastically reduced).

The Ground: Deciding Where to Put Raised Beds

Any blank, sunny space will work. But the question I get asked most often about building a raised bed is, can I build it on top of grass, or do I need to till up the grass? No need to kill the grass—the raised bed will do it for you.

Potatoes in straw

The Frame

Your raised bed frame should be made of untreated wood and should be free. In my garden I use regular 2 × 4 pine lumber for everything except beds for potatoes and carrots, which must be deeper. (I grow my potatoes in straw. You can read about that in my first Forgotten Skills book). No matter where you live, every day thousands of dollars of used but still useful lumber is thrown away. To get free wood to build your frames, ask friends and neighbors. Ask at church or at school. Or use freecycle.org or the free section of Craig's List to ask for clean used lumber. I have not paid for a single stick of the lumber I have used to build my extensive raised bed garden. You shouldn't either.

The Height

If your climate is arid, your raised beds should be as low as possible. This will allow the roots of your plants to access the native soil, which naturally conserves water in summer heat. Native soil "banks" water. If your climate is wet, raised beds will help prevent root rot and diseases associated with undrained soil.

The Lining

Lining the bottom of your frame is essential for keeping out weeds. You can use organic weed fabric, which is made out of paper and meant to dissolve within a year. But that costs money. Here are some free or nearly free solutions:

- Paper bags from the grocery store.
- Newspaper. Ink, by law, is nontoxic and vegetable based, so you don't have to worry about the ink. However, glossy newspaper has been treated with a chemical that you don't want in your garden, so be sure to use only newspaper that does not have a gloss.
- Kraft paper. Brown craft paper makes a great liner and can be purchased in rolls pretty cheaply or even at dollar stores. A huge roll, called "contractor's paper," is available at Home Depot and Lowe's stores for ten dollars. If you are using paper, use a lot.
- If you have problems with weeds that spread by roots under the ground, like pasture grass, line your beds with professional-quality weed barrier from your local garden center. One or two layers will do the job. Cut a small hole (size of your hand) in the center so that worms can access your raised bed—this will make the bed healthier.
- Don't use any liner that contains glue or chemicals. Cardboard is glued together, so don't use any cardboard.

The Filling

Filling your raised box should not cost you a dime. The best "fillers" are pine needles, tree leaves, clean grass clippings, straw, and hay. Fill the box to the top, and then some. At least four inches above the top. You'll want to walk or jump on your box after you've added the filler to tamp it down as much as possible, but all this organic material is still going to begin to "melt" over the next few months, so if you fill your box at least four inches above the top, it will be about right by the time the filler has decomposed into compost.

Question: How on earth am I going to be able to grow anything in a box made of 2 × 4s and filled with pine needles?

Answer: Have faith. I know it seems like failure waiting to happen, but it is not. I've done this many times. Once you begin to water your boxes, the filler will immediately begin to decompose and slowly compact. The pine needles, leaves, grass clipping, hay or straw will absorb and hold water, and the roots of the baby plants will happy grow down into it. As you watch all this happen—and as your plants thrive growing in a bed of pine needles—you will think to yourself, "That Caleb Warnock—humble, wise, and charming—sure knows his stuff!" And you will be right.

HAVE FAITH. I KNOW IT SEEMS LIKE FAILURE WAITING TO HAPPEN, BUT IT IS NOT. I'VE DONE THIS MANY TIMES.

Question: What if I can't find any free filler, or I just want to buy soil to fill my boxes?

Answer: Your money, your life. If you can't find any free filler, where do you live? I can't imagine not being able to find people who want to get rid of leaves and grass clippings.

The Topping

After you have heaped your raised bed so that it is more than full with filler, you will need to put a half-inch layer of compost on top or a large handful of compost in every spot you intend to plant seeds. You can use your own homemade compost, or you can get a bag of organic compost from your hardware store.

Planting Your New Box

Plant and water as you would any garden. Corn, beets, onions, and other shallow root vegetables will do fine.

Question: You said carrots and potatoes should be in a deep box. How deep? Do I fill it differently?

Answer: For carrots and potatoes, your box will need to be ten to twelve inches deep.

For carrots: The entire box will need to be filled with rock-free compost if you want straight, thick carrots. Better yet, use a mix of half compost and half sand. Make sure the sand and compost are well mixed.

For potatoes: I strongly recommend growing either in straw or a layer of compost with straw on top. My recent garden tests have proven that you will get double the yield of potatoes if you put the seed potatoes (or peels with eyes) in the bottom of the box and cover them with a mix of half sand and half compost, enough to fill the bottom third of the box. Fill the rest with straw.

Question: How do you rotate your carrots and potatoes if they have to stay in just your tall raised beds?

Answer: Rotating where you plant your vegetables each year helps reduce disease in the garden. Gardens should be rotated on a four-year schedule or longer, meaning you don't plant the same type of vegetable in the same spot for at least four years. When my straw potatoes are done, I move the straw to the compost pit. Then I fill the potato bed up so I can now use it to grow carrots, filling the bed with a new mix of half compost and half sand, using compost I make on my own property. To rotate my potatoes into my former carrot bed, I remove the top two-thirds of the compost and use it to top off other beds or to top off new beds. I plant my potatoes in the bottom third of the compost that is left, and then fill the rest with straw. Especially with potatoes, it is essential to rotate them every year so you don't encourage disease to build up in the soil—and it will, if you don't rotate.

Watering Your Raised Box

I use a single overhead oscillating sprinkler. Mine cost ten dollars at the local hardware store, and it waters the entire garden space. I screwed the sprinkler onto the top of a 4 × 4 piece of lumber that I stuck in the ground so it was about four feet high. This allows the water to get over the corn and every other tall vegetable as the summer goes on. Then I water about once every eight to ten days overnight—a good, deep watering.

Question: What about using drip lines? Everyone uses drip lines. They are so waterwise, surely you use them. (Followed by more inane gushing about the wonders of drip lines. Can you see where this is going?)

Answer: Never. I hate drip lines, and I can't believe people are still using them, although their popularity had begun to fall off dramatically. This is because drip lines clog so easily—even the new supposedly less cloggy kind—and they cost hundreds of dollars to install.

Question: But what about watering? My garden won't make it ten days without water. It will die.

Answer: You are wrong, with two exceptions. First, if your raised beds are tall, you are going to have to water more often. (Even my carrots and potatoes in twelve-inch-tall beds get watered only every eight to ten days, however, and I've had no problems with them.) Second, if your temperature goes above about 110 degrees, you are going to need to water about every five days.

Edible (Chemical-Free) Weedkiller for Garden Pathways

Unfortunately, weeds still grow in the pathways around raised beds, which has been a source of frustration for me for years. So I decided to do something about it. Something I believe is truly revolutionary. After five years of work, thousands of dollars, hundreds of experiments, and hundreds of hours of testing, I am pleased to say that I have formulated an entirely edible backyard weedkiller that is guaranteed to kill all backyard weeds—including the roots—in one application when applied as directed.

My belief is that this recipe has the potential to change the world. With this recipe, I cannot see any reason to use any chemical weedkiller.

My weedkiller . . .

- Is entirely edible. The recipe doubles as a super-healthy salad dressing, which is how I would suggest you eat it.

Cabbage in a bed

- Kills all common backyard weeds in one application when applied as directed.
- Is guaranteed safe for pets, bees, and insects so long as you don't apply it directly on them.
- Is safe and even beneficial for garden soil.
- Is safe for use around children and safe for the person applying the weedkiller (except that you could hurt your eyes if you got it directly in your eyes. Do not get the formula in your eyes.)
- Where I live, the ingredients, when purchased at a grocery store, cost just less than \$3.50 per gallon to make at home. One gallon will kill roughly one hundred to four hundred square feet of weeds, depending on the height and density.
- Can be all natural and 100 percent organic, depending on the quality of vegetables you purchase to make it.
- Will kill living weeds of all ages, and is guaranteed to kill field bindweed, mallow, cheatgrass, dandelions, dock, lawn grass, clover, broadleaf grass, perennial weeds, and all common backyard weeds in a single application when used as directed.
- My recipe does not use salt and will not affect future plantings or have any negative or long-term affect on your soil or garden.
- My recipe takes less than five minutes to make. You will need a blender.
- My weedkiller recipe will also kill vegetables, berry bushes, flowers, and shrubs if applied directly on them. Apply only to plants you wish to kill. This weedkiller may also kill insects if applied directly on them.

It is no exaggeration when I say that creating this formula has required five years of work,

Brussels sprouts

thousands of dollars, hundreds of experiments, and hundreds of hours of testing. Because of all this expense and effort, I cannot give this recipe away. The recipe is available for purchase at SeedRenaissance.com. You need only to purchase the recipe once to use it for your lifetime. My recipe is guaranteed to work with a thirty-day money-back guarantee.

Overwintering Your Raised Bed

Because I have written a popular book about how to garden in winter without artificial heat or electricity in any climate, called *Backyard Winter Gardening*, I get asked a lot whether you can use the raised beds you used in summer for winter gardening too. The answer is yes. I put cold frames and cloches on my shallow raised beds for lots of happy fresh winter eating.

If you don't want to winter garden (What's wrong with you? It's so easy—no bugs, no heat, no work, almost no watering—just picking fresh food!), then I recommend, if you live in the western United States, you plant peas in every available garden space in the fall. Peas fix nitrogen in the soil, and most soil in the West is always nitrogen deficient. Soils in the East are nitrogen deficient only in certain circumstances based on rainfall and other factors. (Sorry, Canadian friends. I have no idea what goes on up there in your soil. Email me and educate me at calebwarnock@yahoo.com). So even if your pea plants never produce peas, they will still fix nitrogen in your soil. And if you use the early-variety peas, you will get to harvest peas in the fall too.

Question: Are there any garden vegetables that won't do well in a raised bed?

Answer: I have grown everything in raised beds. I do use some regular garden ground too, but that is a lot of weeding. Wheat does best in clay soil, and I grow my winter wheat in my pathways and my summer wheat in raised boxes filled with native clay soil that I dug up from more than two feet below ground so I could get it as free of weed seed as possible.

Question: How sturdy do I have to make the raised boxes?

Answer: I wouldn't use one-inch-thick pine boards because they will warp pretty quickly. Use regular 2 × 4s; 4 × 4s are even better.

Question: When are the times to use a box and when will I be okay with the good old-fashioned ground?

Answer: The ground is always going to be a victim of the weed seed bank. I use the good old-fashioned ground when I run out of box space or when I want to do really large plantings, of wheat and corn for example. To make the most of the good old-fashioned ground, use my Edible Weedkiller recipe, as mentioned earlier in this chapter.

Question: Are the screws or nails going to rust? Will they hold if the box starts rotting?

Answer: If you buy the right screws, they will not rust. They need to be outdoor-rated screws. The wood will begin to rot over the years, but using two-inch long screws put into predrilled holes without cracking the wood will make the boxes last at least twice as long. Untreated pine garden boxes in an arid climate could last as long as twenty years. In a humid climate, they will go soft faster. Remember that my boxes are all doing great, and all of them were made with free wood that was old and weatherworn to begin with. Some of my boxes are made from wood that had been sitting outside for two decades or more before it was given to me. When they do need to be replaced, it is cheap and easy—and you can usually lift the old box off without much trouble and build the new box right round the existing soil fill.

Carrots in a bed

Good-bye Garden Pests

Whenever someone contacts me for advice about a garden pest, I ask them two questions:

1. Is your garden no-till? If you are tilling, that is pretty much a guarantee that you will have soil- and plant-borne diseases.
2. Not to be flippant, but are the pests pesky enough to worry about? Meaning, don't panic if you found a single tomato worm. If you are harvesting tomatoes, then you are meeting your goal. If your tomato harvest is threatened by an army of tomato worms, then you should think about taking action. But most of the time, the pests are just not causing enough problems to be panicking over them.

If you have soil diseases, the most likely cause is tilling. In soil that is all-natural, meaning it has not been disturbed by humans, soil diseases with enough oomph to cause real problems are extremely rare. Why? Because Mother Nature has her own health insurance plan for the soil. It works like this: The good and beneficial stuff in the soil outcompetes the bad stuff (bacterias and yeasts), keeping the bad stuff in check. When the good stuff thrives, the bad stuff struggles to colonize. (Interestingly, this is exactly the pattern that Mother Nature follows in the human gut, which must be populated with good bacterias and yeasts in order for us to digest food properly. If we are healthy, the good guys keep the bad guys in check).

When we leave the soil alone with a no-till design, the soil has the best chance to follow Mother Nature's natural plan for health. If we get out of her way, she will take care of most of our garden problems.

Here are some other troubleshooting ideas:

1 **Overwatering.** If you have any soil- or plant-borne diseases, overwatering is one of the main causes. You want your soil to be dry on top most of the time, with the water inside the soil. If you live in a humid area, you need to have good drainage. If you live in an arid climate, you need to reduce your drip system or change your watering plan.

2 **Dirty garden.** Both diseases and pests love to hide in the moist soil under dead leaves and other dead and rotting organic material. If you have organic debris piling up in the garden and a pest invasion, it is a good sign that you need to do a little tidying up. Dead and dying leaves and spent plants go into the compost pile or preferably the compost pit (see my book on pit composting for details).

3 **Rotation.** Disease and pests are often plant-specific, meaning that they are attracted to a specific type of crop. The longer a crop grows in the same place, the more those diseases and pests flock to and colonize the area. They reproduce and set up permanent residence. This is one of two reasons that we rotate our garden crops. As a general rule of thumb, you should only grow the same thing in the same space every fifth year. For example, when you grow tomatoes, do not plant tomatoes in that same area again for four years. This rotation schedule should not be by vegetable but by family of vegetables. For example, brassicas are all in the same family—broccoli, cauliflower, kale, cabbage, Brussels sprouts, and collards. If you grow cabbages one year, and then grow broccoli in that same spot the next year, you have not really "rotated" your crop because you have planted the same family of vegetable in the same spot, and pests are usually attracted to everyone in the same family. It is much better to grow your melons where you grew your brassicas, and then grow your corn there in the third year, then put your beans there in the fourth year, then put flowers there in the fifth year, for example.

4 **Fallow.** If you have a true problem with a specific pest or disease, and you have diligently done the first three things on this list, then it is time to start moving to more drastic measures. The first of these is to let the land lie fallow. This means that you simply keep it blank for a year—plant nothing, and do not allow weeds to grow. The concept here is that whenever you are growing something, your soil is working, and working hard. Your soil likes to work. But sometimes the only way to heal is to rest, and lying fallow is how soil rests. So plant nothing in your problem area, and keep it clear of weeds too, for a whole year. You can continue to grow in the other areas of the garden.

5 **Solarize.** In extreme circumstances—especially in cases of pest invasion—if you have tried the first four items on this list and still have a problem, the answer might be solarization. This means that you let the soil lie fallow while also covering it with a sheet of plastic. You can try this for two weeks and see if it solves your problem. Another even more

effective method is to heavily douse the area with common grocery store vinegar (white or apple cider), and then cover it with plastic and solarize it for two weeks. If after two weeks you still have problems, apply more vinegar and solarize for the rest of the summer and try again the next year. Remember to clean the land before you solarize. No weeds, no leaves—no organic material where bugs and spores can hide.

Dealing with Aphids

Aphids are a plague pretty much everywhere. They love brassicas especially and will usually attack those first. Here are several strategies for dealing with aphids:

1. Don't overwater.

2. Do not let spent leaves and other dying organic material pile up in the garden.

3. Aphids often show up first in brassicas—broccoli, collards, cauliflower, kale, Brussels sprouts, cabbages, kohlrabi, and so on. Our goal is to harvest our brassicas before the aphids overrun them. If your brassicas are not ready to harvest and are infested with aphids, that is a pretty good sign that you planted your brassicas too late in the season. It is also a strong sign that you purchased your brassicas as starts from a nursery. Garden nurseries are almost always vectors for aphids and other plant pests, but especially aphids. Anything you bring home from a nursery is likely to spread aphids—early-season flowers often have them, for example. This is why serious gardeners usually try to grow their own

from seed instead of bringing things from a nursery. Remember that most of the country does not have a long enough growing season to plant brassicas from seed, so they must be started indoors. But most people don't move them outside soon enough. Brassicas are cool-weather plants, and they don't love the heat of summer. Brassicas are most healthy—and least likely to be infested with aphids—if they are started from seed in January and put out into the garden in a cold frame or cloche as soon as the soil can be worked (meaning the ground has thawed). This way, they will quickly develop a strong root system, and by the time aphid season arrives, you should have already harvested your brassicas, pulled out the remaining plant material, and put it in the compost pit or pile. Never leave brassica plant material in the garden after harvesting, because it will be a magnet and nursery for aphids.

4. I have done a lot of experimenting over the years, and I have found that aphids love, and I do mean *love*, one plant in particular: tai sai. Tai sai is an Asian green that is fast growing. One of the best ways to control aphids is to feed them what they love, believe it or not. I plant what I call "sacrificial tai sai" in my garden, and the aphids are always drawn to it first. I let them infest the plant, and then I pull up the whole plant and burn it completely or seal it in a plastic bag, leave it in full sun for three days to "cook," and then throw it in the trash without opening it. Sacrificial tai sai actually works really well, and I sell the seeds at SeedRenaissance.com. You will need succession plantings, meaning that you plant new seeds about every two weeks so that you always have a new crop of it coming on to draw the aphids. You only need a few plants at a time. Sacrificial tai sai also works very well in cold frames and greenhouses. It's great "pest control" for greenhouses. As soon as the aphids colonize the plant, carefully pull up the whole plant, root and all, and treat it as described above.

I HAVE DONE A LOT OF EXPERIMENTING OVER THE YEARS, AND I HAVE FOUND THAT APHIDS LOVE, AND I DO MEAN *LOVE*, ONE PLANT IN PARTICULAR: TAI SAI.

5. If you have an infestation that threatens your crop—in your greenhouse, for example, or on your Brussels sprouts—spray them with a dilution of my Edible Weedkiller Recipe, available at SeedRenaisssance.com. Remember it must be diluted, because you don't want to kill the plant, just the aphids. Dilute the prepared weedkiller recipe two-to-one—for example, one cup of edible weedkiller and two cups of hot water. Spray this onto the plants that are infested with aphids. Spray heavily, taking care to get up under the leaves and all around the stems. Then wait three days and spray again, to get the last of the little bugs. That should kill them all and allow you to harvest. If you find that you have aphids on the broccoli that you have just harvested, for example, soak them in the dilution for at least an hour, then wash vigorously before eating. This dilution is also effective at killing pests that threaten fruit trees (at least it has been at my house).

Bug Prevention

There are some organic methods, widely practiced, that help ensure that you never get an insect invasion in your garden in the first place. They both have to do with chickens.

1 **Chicken tractor.** Before I explain the bug part of this, let me explain the concept. If you put a few chickens in a small protected and confined area with access to the native soil, they will scratch it up completely, essentially

tilling it for you. *But wait, Caleb! You said not to till!* I can hear you saying it. Many people have said it to me already. But "chicken tilling" has nothing in common with mechanical tilling. Chickens till only the surface, which does not disturb the natural soil fertility web but does kill the weeds. Chickens also fertilize as they go, if you get my drift. A "chicken tractor" just means a mobile chicken enclosure that can be moved to a new location about once a week through summer, when the chickens inside have cleared the land you want cleared. (How often it needs to be moved depends on how large it is and the number of chickens inside.) Here is the pest control part—you can build a small chicken tractor, sized to fit in your garden paths. The chickens will eat every bug and larvae they come across in the soil as you move the tractor slowly around the garden paths. This is natural pest control at its best. Why not just let the chickens loose in the garden, you ask? Because they will destroy everything. They will dig up every bed and peck every tomato, squash, and cucumber. You don't want them to have free access to the garden.

Broccoli, a brassica

2 **Chicken moat.** A variation of this concept is to build a permanent chicken run around your garden, or around some of your garden. For example, you build a fenced "run" on three or four sides of your garden. Because all garden bugs move—and because chickens will eat every bug and larvae they can find—this greatly cuts down on the pests in the garden by creating a "moat" of chicken protection to surround your plants. The moat can be just three to four feet wide, but the fence should be high enough to ensure that the chickens don't get into the garden.

There is a caution in dealing with chicken tractors and chicken moats. If you are overfeeding the chickens, they will ignore the insects and larvae and just luxuriate in the food you give them. In the summer, chickens with access to open ground need very little feed—very little. If chickens are in a moat or tractor, you should be able to cut their feed back by at least 80 percent, if not to zero.

A couple of last notes on pest management in the garden:

All around the United States, the University Extension Service has experts on hand, in

Garter snake

every state, to help gardeners diagnose pests and diseases at no cost. Some states are better than others for offering organic solutions to these problems, however. Some Extension professionals are openly hostile to organic gardening in general. (Do you sense the voice of experience speaking?) But your local Extension Service will have no problem helping you identify exactly what your pest or disease is. If it cannot offer you a suitable organic solution, go online to your local organic gardening community or Facebook page and ask for help. You can usually find these people by typing the name of your area and the words "organic gardening" or "permaculture" into the Facebook search feature.

Not everything that is labeled "organic" is safe, nor does it support the idea of do-no-harm gardening methods. Diatomaceous earth is one of those things. Diatomaceous earth can permanently damage your lungs when inhaled, and also damages the lungs of children and pets. In my view, it is just too dangerous to use—it's not worth the risk of lung cancer and asthma. Read the warning labels for yourself, and do the research. It's dangerous stuff. If you have problems with slugs or other pests, garden snakes are a great option. Wait! Don't run off. Garden snakes, also called garter snakes, never have teeth—ever. They are perfectly safe, and they love to eat slugs and bugs by the dozens, every single day. You can also find instructions on the Internet for beer traps and honey traps for slugs. There are ways to deal with slugs without diatomaceous earth. At the very least, if you are going to use diatomaceous earth, wear a face mask and keep the children and pets away, and don't do it on a windy day.

Asian Greens

(Chinese Mustards)

Brassica rapa | Annual

Asian greens have many overlooked benefits and uses. They are nutrient dense. They grow rapidly, generally tolerate cold soil, and love a greenhouse, cold frame, cloche, or row cover, making them a standard for fresh greens in a winter garden. They have a good flavor, and one of my favorite things about them is that they often have a crunchy texture when mature, or at least have stems with crunch, and I like vegetables that crunch because they make you feel like you are actually eating substantial food. Another benefit—if you have a pet rabbit, like we do—rabbits love this stuff, which makes it easy to feed your rabbit self-sufficiently year-round. Asian greens are great as sauté or in stir-fry, curry, salads, or green smoothies.

This group covers a range of root and leafy vegetables: Napa cabbage, won bok, bok choi, pak choi, choi sum, tai sai (totsoi), mizuna, Michihili Chinese Cabbage, broccoli raab (but not broccoli), and more. The varieties listed here are available at SeedRenaissance.com

When to plant: All Asian greens can be planted as soon as the soil can be worked in spring, but it may be weeks before they germinate. Asian greens can also be planted in late summer or early autumn for fall harvesting.

Where to plant: In clay or loam.

How to plant: Seeds are covered with a quarter-inch of soil and kept moist until germination.

How to fertilize: Not necessary.

Transplanting: Not necessary.

When to harvest: Leaves can be harvested at any size.

How to preserve: Asian greens are eaten fresh and are generally not preserved.

RECOMMENDED VARIETIES

- **Chinese Cabbage Michihili:** Excellent fall and winter greens. Keep outdoors for fall and in a greenhouse or cold frame for winter. In winter, this cabbage is not likely to form a full head. Harvest the leaves for salads and Asian-inspired dishes. It is light-to-medium green in color. The mature leaves can be giant—twenty-four inches or more in the right conditions.

- **Mizuna:** This Asian green is a winter wonder; it pops up in my geothermal greenhouse despite the cold nights, and it grows very fast—even in January. It grows more prolifically and more reliably than other winter greens. Cut at ground level, and it will grow back over and over. The bright green, frizzy leaves are just fun to look at, and it's great for salads and green smoothies. Leaves can get up to ten inches long but taste best when smaller and younger.

- **Purple Top Globe Turnip:** Turnips will be covered in another section of this book, but it is worth noting here that turnip greens (the leaves) are quite edible, especially in the young stages and in cool weather. If you are going to eat them raw, you'll want them young because sometimes the older leaves, especially in hot weather as the plant begins to bolt to seed, will develop a spiny sort of hair on them that isn't palatable. These can be sautéed, put into quiche, yakisoba, stir-fry, salads, or green smoothies. The serrated leaves can be two feet tall but taste best when young. The color of the leaves ranges from gray-green to medium green.

- **Komatsuna:** This Japanese vegetable grows very fast in cold soil, making it ideal for winter cold frames, hot beds, and greenhouses. This is about a week slower than mizuna and has a nice flavor. Cut at ground level and it will grow back over and over. It is bright green and is great for salads, smoothies, and so on.

- **Sacrificial Tai Sai:** (organic pest control): This Asian green works better than any other in my trials of sacrificial plants (you can read more about this on page 52). It's one of the best organic methods for dealing with slugs and aphids. Simply let them flock to this plant, which they love, so they will leave your other plants alone. This works like magic, especially in greenhouses, cold frames, and hot beds—and in the open garden. And I haven't even mentioned yet that this vegetable is quite delicious, fast-growing, loves cool weather, is great for greenhouses, and cold frames.

Asparagus

Asparagus officinalis | Perennial

We grow asparagus all wrong, and we need to change. In history, this delicacy was not necessarily a backyard vegetable. Instead it was what today we would call a "food forest" vegetable. The concept of food forests used to be a way of life. These were public or common lands, especially in rural communities around the world, where naturalized (perennial or self-seeding) food grew without anyone's help and could be harvested by anyone who knew where to find it.

Asparagus was one of these, and settlers across the United States planted beds of asparagus that can still be found today—if you can get anyone to tell you where they are. I grew up with access to one of these century-old asparagus beds, planted by the pioneers who settled the Utah desert and made it bloom with food and flowers. Before my grandfather died, he asked me to keep the location of this asparagus bed a secret, and I have. Despite being several hundred yards long, this bed is already fully harvested each year, and there simply will never be "room" for more people to harvest here. I have a friend who has bugged me for several years, wanting me to tell her where she can find this bed of asparagus. When I asked her permission to run a piece of her writing on my blog (CalebWarnock.blogspot.com) as a guest post, she tried to blackmail me (in good humor) for the information.

"Will you tell me the secret location of the wild-growing asparagus?" she messaged me on Facebook.

"Yes," I messaged back. "But you might get shot trying to harvest it. It's private property. And my family often shoots first and then asks questions."

"I own Kevlar. And a gun," she replied.

Of course this conversation was meant to be funny. No one is going to really shoot anyone, but the location is truly a guarded secret. Rather than subterfuge and secrets, there is a better way—we should plant more of these public asparagus beds. What a gift

to the future! One day, after I have graduated from this mortal life, I hope to meet the person or people who took the time and effort to plant the asparagus I grew up with. Their names have been lost from memory and history. The irrigation ditches where they grow were dug in 1908, and I suspect someone planted that asparagus soon thereafter. Whoever they were, they have blessed generations of lives.

There is some discussion, when it comes to asparagus, about whether it is best to plant from seeds or crowns. I have tried both, and I find that seeds work better because planting crowns is a bit labor intensive. You have to plant them deep in loamy soil and then keep burying them as they come up. If you buy crowns, follow the directions that come with them. If someone is nice enough to give you crowns from their property to transplant, try to leave them in the soil they are growing in—in other words, don't shake off all the dirt because this puts the roots and crown into shock. Give them generous water the first year. If you are getting bare-root crowns from a store or garden center, check them carefully to make sure they have not dried out and died. If they are not moist in the store, they are likely dead. Crowns are supposed to be "faster" than planting asparagus from seed, but in my experience, crowns go through so much shock that they often die or are already dead in the store and almost never produce better than seeds. Crowns are first bare-root harvested, stuck into plastic bags,

RECOMMENDED VARIETIES

- **Mary Washington Asparagus:** Known for its long, thick spears, productivity, and flavor, as well as its ability to hold its flavor when frozen—if you can stop yourself from eating it immediately. This variety is a favorite for flavor.

shipped great distances, left on store shelves, and then taken home by someone and planted in "real" conditions, which the crowns (often grown in nurseries) have never experienced before. Seeds are much cheaper than crowns, and I think they are easier to deal with. That's my two cents, but there will never be a "right" answer. They both work if you are smart and careful about where you get your crowns and how and when you plant them. Never plant crowns so early in the year that the soil might freeze on them, but you also can't plant them so late that the soil is too warm for them. They like cool soil.

When to plant: In spring as seeds, crowns, or root cuttings.

Where to plant: In loamy soil with good drainage and regular access to water. Make sure you plant asparagus where you want it forever, because it will likely outlive you.

How to plant: Plant root cuttings in a foot-deep trench. Plant seeds one inch deep.

How to fertilize: Asparagus is not generally fertilized, as you don't want to encourage it to bolt (go to seed too fast).

How to transplant: Root cuttings can be carefully removed with a razor knife from mature plants. Entire plants (called root crowns when they don't have foliage) can be dug up and moved to your garden if you can find someone willing to give you some from their garden. My understanding is that in some parts of the eastern United States, wild asparagus is so common that you get the plants readily, but that is not true in the West where I live.

When to harvest: Early summer, just as the asparagus emerges from the ground and is tender. Do not harvest plants that are younger than three years old, as it may kill them. Only mature plants should be harvested.

Basil

Ocimum basilicum | Annual

Sweet basil is probably the most popular culinary herb in the United States, and with good reason. The flavor and aroma of fresh basil are beyond compare. Basil can also be frustrating to people like me, who love it and want to produce enough to be "self-reliant," meaning I don't have to buy it at the store. Why? Because when fresh basil is dried, it nearly vanishes. This is not true of all herbs. Oregano, for example, is fairly substantial when dried. But when I dry a huge quantity of fresh basil from my garden for winter use, by the time it is dry, there is almost nothing there. No matter how much basil I grow each year, I have never been able to harvest for a whole year of use. I always have to start buying it mid-winter.

Two more cautions about basil: In arid climates, it likes partial sun in summer, and in partial sun it will double or triple in size. It will not do as well if it is exposed to direct sun all summer. Finally, basil can be victim to many diseases, including wilt, stem blight, and leaf spots. In summer, I try to walk through my garden once a day to check things, and basil is one of the reasons this is necessary. The moment you see any problems with your basil, harvest all the plants, discarding any affected leaves. It is much better to harvest earlier and harvest fewer leaves than it is to lose the whole crop.

When to plant: After all threat of frost has passed. However . . .

I do extensive winter-garden testing of seed to try to reclaim lost knowledge about what will grow in cold soil conditions. The results are often surprising. For example, who knew that Dragon Tongue Bush Beans have cold soil tolerance? Perhaps the most surprising and frustrating test I have ever done was planting basil seed in January in my geothermal greenhouse. In January where I live at 5,200 feet, the temperature is often below

freezing twenty-four hours a day, sometimes for weeks at a stretch in January. Nevertheless, I have learned the hard way that the only way to know for sure if a seed is cold-soil tolerant is to test it. So I planted basil seed in January, and to my shock it germinated within a week. I was very excited, and checked the tiny little seedlings every day, waiting for them to sprout their second set of leaves (called true leaves).

I waited for four months.

Four months! Those darn little seedlings just sat there, not growing, not dying. I tried cloching them with a glass bell jar to add natural heat, to no avail. I have never had another test like this one. Usually my cold-soil germination tests end in one of three ways—the seeds sprout, or they don't, or they sprout and grow a bit and die from cold. Basil is the only vegetable I've ever tested, out of hundreds and hundreds of varieties (cultivars) that simply sat there and refused to grow or die. Go figure. What this may mean is that basil could grow in a cloche in a hot bed (not a plain winter greenhouse or cold frame), either in the open garden or in the greenhouse in winter. But I have not tested that theory yet. Basil is one of the vegetables we use the most at our house, so it would surely be nice to extend the fresh harvest, if possible. Meanwhile, it is entirely possible to easily grow basil over winter in a pot in a sunny window in your house.

Where to plant: Basil prefers loamy soil but will tolerate some clay or sand.

How to plant: Barely cover the tiny seeds with soil, and keep moist until germination.

How to fertilize: Not necessary in good soil.

How to transplant: When the plants are at least an inch tall, dig up the plant, root and all, and transplant it where you want it. Once settled in its new home, water deeply and immediately.

When to harvest: Leaves can be picked at any size. The top leaves of any branch of this plant should be harvested as soon as possible because this will encourage the lower branches to leaf out, producing a larger plant and a larger harvest. Basil plants will continue to grow vigorously all summer if you take no more than a third of the leaves at any one time. Harvest all of the leaves just before the first frost of autumn and dry them for winter use.

How to preserve: Leaves can be dried whole and stored for winter use in a bag or bottle. Leaves can be pureed in water and frozen in ice cube trays for later use. If frozen in ice, be sure to triple-bag the ice cubes when they are done to avoid a freezer-burned flavor.

RECOMMENDED VARIETIES

- **Sweet Basil (*Ocimum basilicum*):** This is the herb we use the most at our house—on pasta and on roast.
- **Cinnamon Basil (*Ocimum basilicum*):** A basil plant with a cinnamon flavor. Fun to grow, and easy to use in any dish where you want a cinnamon flavor. May be used dried or fresh. Plant directly in the garden after all danger of frost has passed or indoors up to four weeks before your last frost date.
- **Lime Basil (*Ocimum americanum*):** A basil plant with a wonderful lime flavor! Fun to grow, and easy to use in any dish where you want a lime flavor. May be used dried or fresh. Plant directly in the garden after all danger of frost has passed or indoors up to four weeks before your last frost date. Please note, this variety does not cross with Sweet Basil or Cinnamon Basil.

Beans

Phaseolus vulgaris | Annual

Recently a seed-saving acquaintance of mine contacted me to say that a man who had been working for years to save some of the rarest beans in the world had died. This friend of mine had traded beans with the man in the past, and his widow had contacted her, unsure what to do with his priceless collection of seeds. Some of these seeds were available nowhere else in the world. My friend immediately contacted me, because I had traded beans with her in the past, and she knew I was an experienced seed-saver. She asked me to please take some of this man's varieties to keep them from extinction. She mailed me seeds from seventeen of his most rare varieties, and all seventeen of these varieties are growing in my garden right now as I write this. Other seed-saving friends around the country took some of his other varieties. For now, it looks as though the work of this man's lifetime will be preserved and kept from extinction, if just barely.

This story raises the tough question that all serious seed savers face—what happens when I die? This question has been particularly vexing to me because I am maintaining dozens of seed lines across many vegetable varieties that are being maintained by absolutely no one else in the world. What happens when I die? I hope this book, and my other books, will help convince people of the value of these seeds and people will purchase the seeds from SeedRenaissance.com, learn how to keep them pure and true, and keep these seed lines from passing from the face of the earth like so many other heirloom seed varieties. Our seed supply—which is our food supply—must remain in the public domain. Only oligarchs and despots win when the seed supply is controlled by "the people in charge" instead of backyard gardeners and independently owned family seed companies.

But back to beans. Why are they valuable? Because they are the "meat" of the vegetable

Dragon Tongue Bush Bean

world, with a big dose of protein that is both healthy and self-reliant. Beans and grains, when eaten together, contain all the amino acids the body needs to thrive. Beans can easily be stored for later use without losing their protein content, much like wheat and other grains.

When to plant: After all danger of frost has passed.

Where to plant: Beans are not picky about soil and do well in clay or loam.

How to plant: One inch deep and about six inches apart for both pole and bush beans.

How to fertilize: Beans benefit from being watered with diluted compost tea or the homemade organic fertilizer listed in this book just as the beans begin to form.

How to transplant: Beans should be planted directly in the garden and not transplanted.

When to harvest: Harvesting beans depends on what your goals are, as listed below:

Green beans: Bean pods that are used as "green beans" are picked as soon as they are several inches long. The sooner they are picked, the more tender they will be. Green beans can be eaten raw or blanched or frozen or canned.

Shelly beans: Beans that are removed from the pod while they are immature (usually green) are called shelly beans. Shelly beans can be eaten raw, much like edamame, and added to soups, or they can be frozen, canned, or served as a side dish.

Dry beans: Beans that are allowed to dry on the vine are removed from the dried pods and stored for later eating or used as seeds for future gardens. Beans should dry fully on the vine. If your beans do not dry fully before the fall rains or winter snow, consider switching to a bean variety with a shorter day-count, as recommended below. Dry beans are used in soups and stews and used to make barbecue beans and refried beans, among many other options. Dry beans can be soaked and cooked on the stove, in a slow cooker, or in a thermal oven. My wife likes to take four cups of soaked dry or shelly beans and add them to a slow cooker with a pound of raw bacon and a quarter cup of molasses. Allow this to cook for several hours on high or overnight on low. Beware—this recipe is addictive!

RECOMMENDED VARIETIES

- **Indian Woman Yellow:** Of over two hundred varieties that I have trialed, this is the earliest to mature while still being hugely prolific. These are moderately sweet, green string beans, sometimes double-stringed. They are easy to grow, producing huge quantities of beans that are great for eating raw, cooked, frozen, or canned. They will stay alive quite awhile in a cold frame, as late as December. This is also the best self-seeding bean I've ever found. These beans were given to me by a woman who attended a speech I gave. The one company in the United States that sold them has dropped them. SeedRenaissance.com is proud to be the only company in the world selling these beans, keeping them from extinction. The dried beans are a rustic yellow color.

- **Pioneer Pink-Eyed Beans:** These have been saved from extinction by one family. I've been looking for this seed for a long time and had come to the conclusion that it was extinct. Over and over again, I would be reading in my pioneer gardening research and the pioneers would list the vegetables they were growing, but often the only variety name they mentioned was pink-eyed beans. It is amazing how many pioneer accounts mention these beans. I'd looked everywhere for them, literally searched up and down, but had not been able to find any anywhere—even in seed banks. And then, one day, I gave a speech, and afterward this beautiful tiny grandmother came up to me and asked if I had ever heard of pink-eyed beans. "Yes, but I've searched everywhere for them, and they are extinct," I said. "I have some," she said. "And since I know you will grow them, I will give them to you." I almost wept. I couldn't believe it. This wonderful woman got the seed from the last known family to grow the seed, and she gave it to me, and even though it was late June, I immediately planted. Thankfully we had a late fall, and all these beans did very well in my garden before the frost in September. They are early bush beans, and they produce the largest common beans I've ever been able to grow—no wonder they were so popular with the pioneers! We cannot let them go extinct. They are too important.

- **Dragon Tongue Bush Bean:** I have learned over the years to test every seed I can get my hands on because you never know when a seed will surprise you. To that end, I did a bean trial in my unheated geothermal greenhouse in January just to see what would happen—and lo and behold, this bean sprouted and grew. I have since tested it in the open garden in cold frames, where it also performs shockingly well. I have been told that this is actually an ancient Scandinavian bean, likely from Denmark, which is why it has this remarkable cold tolerance. This is also the second earliest bean to produce in side-by-side summer tests, and definitely the most beautiful bean I grow—a pale green bean with jagged purple streaks. It produces a lot of beans, and the beans are thick. They are not good for eating raw, but they are great when cooked. It also makes a good-sized shelling bean.

- **Broad Windsor Fava Bean:** This remarkable fava (lima bean) has been grown in cold weather for centuries as a "hunger gap" food for both people and animals. It can be planted outside as soon as the soil can be worked in spring. You will be amazed to watch these beans grow even as temperatures dip below freezing at night, and they have been in full flower despite being covered with snow on many occasions in my garden. They produce huge, thick pods just as summer is starting—at about the same time you typically plant your common garden beans. The shelly beans are often the size of a quarter! These beans also do very well in the greenhouse when planted in January. This is an old English heritage bean. It is great for eating (peel the inner shell off each fresh bean) and also an excellent way to help feed your chickens self-sufficiently. It is a reliable self-seeder, both in the backyard garden and in the greenhouse.

Beets

Beta vulgaris | Biennial

The key to loving beets is to branch out. Are you only familiar with those dark red beets that drip juice everywhere and are only good for pickling and making borscht? Congratulations! You have a whole new food experience ahead of you in the form of sugar beets, golden beets, and chioggia beets. When I do tasting classes from my autumn garden, I always include sugar beets because most people have never tasted them, and they are blown away. Golden beets are wonderful and don't taste like traditional red beets, and chioggia beets are among my favorites because of their beauty and flavor. If you don't think a beet can be beautiful, you've never seen a chioggia!

One of the most commonly overlooked aspects of beets is the greens. Beet greens can be picked fresh for salads at any time or cooked as greens. They are tender and succulent. Beet greens are also perfect for greenhouse growing. They thrive in my winter geothermal greenhouse, (you can read about my greenhouse in my *Backyard Winter Gardening* book.)

When to plant: You can begin planting as soon as the ground can be worked in spring and continue succession plantings through mid-summer for fall harvesting.

Where to plant: Beets aren't picky. They do well in heavy clay soils and lighter loamy soils.

How to plant: Plant the seeds up to an inch deep.

How to fertilize: It is not necessary to fertilize beets if you have good soil.

How to transplant: Beets don't like to be transplanted. They should be sown directly in the garden soil.

When to harvest: Any time after the root has formed a bulb. If you let the bulb get much larger than a baseball, you run the real risk of letting your beets go woody.

How to preserve: Pick ripe beets, cut the tops off, and store in damp sand, sawdust, or pine shavings in a cool dark place, such as a garage, basement cold room, or cellar. The beets will slowly produce edible leaves in the dark, which are delicious in salads, and you can eat these preserved beets at any time through autumn and winter.

Chioggia beet

RECOMMENDED BEET VARIETIES

- **Albino Sugar Beets**: Hundreds of you have tasted these beets at my classes, and thousands of you have read about me making sugar with these beets in my *Forgotten Skills of Self-Sufficiency* book. These seeds are difficult to find, which is why they are among the bestsellers at SeedRenaisssance.com. If you have never tasted a sugar beet, you are in for a huge surprise—they taste like no other beet in the world. These pure white beets can be eaten just like any other beet—raw for a snack, raw in salads, baked, or cooked in soups and stews. This is one of my top ten must-have vegetables!

- **Chioggia Beets:** These old Italian heirlooms are my favorite red beets in the world. Why? Because they never bleed all over, they are stunning when cut open (as you can see on the left), and they are sweet and crisp. They don't taste at all like a traditional red beet—the flavor is a blend of sugar beet and traditional beet. They are great for eating raw as slices or for salads or for cooking. I love these!

- **Golden Beets**: These century-old American heirlooms are an orangey-gold color and have a mild, delicate flavor that stands out in roasted vegetable dishes and looks great in salads and served as a side dish. These are simply great!

Broccoli

Brassica oleracea | Biennial

Broccoli is a cool-weather plant and doesn't love the heat of summer. Broccoli does best when started from seed in January and then transplanted out into the garden in a cold frame, cloche, or row cover as soon as the soil can be worked (meaning the ground has thawed). This way, it will quickly develop a strong root system and produce in the cool season instead of summer. It is always best to grow a short-season (short day count) variety (cultivar) of broccoli so that you have the best chance of harvesting before aphid season starts. Aphids love broccoli, and our goal is to harvest before the aphids overrun them. If your broccoli is not ready to harvest before they are infested with aphids, that is a pretty good sign that you planted your broccoli too late in the season. It is also a strong sign that you purchased your broccoli as starts from a nursery. Garden nurseries are almost always vectors for aphids. This is why serious gardeners usually try to grow their own from seed instead of bringing things from a nursery. Remember that most of the country does not have a long enough growing season to plant brassicas from seed, so they must be started indoors. But most people don't move them outside soon enough. By the time aphid season arrives, you should have already harvested your broccoli, pulled out the remaining plant material, and put it in the compost pit or pile. Never leave broccoli plant material in the garden after harvesting, because it will be a magnet and nursery for aphids.

Broccoli plants have two harvests. The first is the main head. Once that head is cut off, smaller side heads will form. If you continue to harvest these at their prime, more will grow. Once the summer heat starts, these side heads will quickly flower and bolt to seed. The flowering heads are still edible and delicious in the young stages, but the stems get woody quickly.

When to plant: All broccoli varieties require a long growing season, often needing two hundred days or more to produce broccoli heads when planted from seed. Few areas of

Early Purple Broccoli

the United States have long enough growing seasons to successfully produce broccoli when directly seeded outdoors. Most of us will need to either buy plants at a nursery or start plants indoors months in advance.

Where to plant: Broccoli is not picky about soil and does well in heavy or loamy soils.

How to plant: If you are starting seeds indoors, plant the seeds three months before you intend to move the plants outside. Seeds should be covered with a quarter-inch of soil and kept damp until sprouting.

How to fertilize: Broccoli does not need fertilizer if you have good soil.

How to transplant: Transplant outdoors in mid-spring. Broccoli transplants are hardy enough to survive light frosts but should be protected from heavy frosts for the first two to three weeks after transplanting.

When to harvest: There is an old saying: "Opportunity is not a lengthy visitor," and this is true of broccoli heads. Tightly packed, beautiful heads of broccoli are in perfect condition for only three to four days After this, they will begin to loosen and spread. Broccoli heads are best picked early, before the flowerheads begin to open. Broccoli is one of the plants you really want to inspect carefully after harvesting. Check carefully on the undersides to see if you have aphids, spiders, caterpillars, worms, or other critters hiding in them. It is always a good idea to immerse your fresh broccoli into a bowl of heavily salted water for several minutes, weighting the head down with a plate or bowl so it doesn't float. Then remove the head, put it on a plate, take it outside, and let it sit for a half hour or more. This puts spiders and other critters hiding in the broccoli on warning and they leave, heading back into the outdoors, where they belong. Unfortunately, you also need to do this with broccoli from the grocery store. I can't tell you how many times I have looked at the fresh broccoli in the store and found worms, aphids, and spiders hiding in the undersides. After immersing in salt water and then taking it outside so the creature can escape, bring the broccoli inside, cut it up carefully, inspecting as you go. After years of finding "friends" in broccoli both fresh and store-bought, I can tell you for sure that I never, ever serve broccoli without carefully inspecting every single piece—and I never eat broccoli at parties or events from the veggie tray without carefully inspecting it either. If you knew how often I found hangers-on, you would be mortified. Sorry to freak you out, but the truth sets you free, I hope.

How to preserve: Blanch and freeze.

RECOMMENDED VARIETIES

- I recommend any heirloom variety with the shortest day count possible. Di Cicco is my favorite, and I try to stock Early Purple at SeedRenaissance.com if I can.

Brussels Sprouts

Brassica oleracea | Biennial

Brussels sprouts can be frustrating because they take so long to produce. I will not lie to you—one year I went to great lengths to harvest the Brussels sprouts from my garden in November and serve them fresh for a large Thanksgiving dinner of extended family. Several family members left them on their plates at the end of dinner and I'm still smarting. They wasted my hard-won Brussels sprouts! I'm a forgiving person, but I can tell you that I have never served my own homegrown at Thanksgiving dinner again. When you grow them yourself, and you hand-cut every *darn* one from the stem, picking off the outer leaves, hand-washing them one at a time, and then prepare them hot and fresh for dinner, glazed in balsamic vinegar, lime juice, and a touch of brown sugar—well, you should fall on your knees with gratitude if someone is willing to go through that work for you.

Pfft. I'm not bitter. Not much!

What were we talking about? Oh yes. For advice on when to plant and how to make sure your harvest is bug-free, please read the advice I give about broccoli—it all applies to Brussels sprouts too.

When to plant: Seeds should be planted indoors or in the greenhouse at least two months, if not three months, before the expected last frost date. Brassica seeds, including Brussels sprouts, like to germinate in cool temperatures. Keep the seed moist until germination, which may take a couple weeks or more inside a greenhouse, where temperatures fluctuate.

Where to plant: In clay or loam.

How to plant: Plant seeds a quarter-inch deep and keep moist until germination.

How to fertilize: Not necessary.

How to transplant: Brussels sprouts can be transplanted outdoors after being hardened off, when they are at least four inches tall. Hardening off means you put the plants outside during the day, but only while the air temperature is above freezing. This should be done for a week before transplanting the starts outdoors and keeping them covered with a cloche or cold frame in March.

When to harvest: Brussels sprouts need to be harvested in cool—or even cold—weather for the best sweet taste. They achieve peak flavor after three mild frosts or one hard frost. The problem with harvesting Brussels sprouts is aphids—the scourge of all brassicas. The key is to control aphids early by spraying a dilution of two to one of Caleb's Guaranteed Edible Weed Killer recipe onto the plants every couple of weeks all summer and once a week during autumn. This will kill the aphids early, before they can colonize on the plants. Another method is to cut down the ripe stalks, spray them at high pressure with the hose, and then cut off each sprout and peel off the outer leaf layers to reveal the clean sprouts beneath. The downside of this method is that, if the infestation is bad, you will often have to peel off half the leaves of a sprout, which is a disheartening waste.

How to preserve: Blanch and freeze.

RECOMMENDED VARIETIES

I recommend any heirloom variety. There are no short day-count varieties of Brussels sprouts. If I ever get any spare time, perhaps I will try to develop one. Or if you know of a rare early Brussels sprouts cultivar, please email me at calebwarnock@yahoo.com.

Cabbage

Brassica oleracea | Biennial

There is really nothing on earth that compares to the sweet flavor of fresh cabbage picked in late autumn after a few good hard frosts. At our house, me and my wife and the grandkids eat it as a crunchy snack. Frost triggers the sweetness in cabbage. A big tight head of cabbage can be divided among several meals. I love shredded cabbage on tacos and chunks of cabbage, rubbed with olive oil, in a pan of roasted vegetables.

When to plant: Success with cabbages is all about day counts. Most of the United States does not have a long enough growing season to start cabbages directly from seed in the garden, despite the fact that cabbage seed can be planted earlier than most vegetables. For success, use a short day-count cabbage like Danish Ballhead, and plant the seeds outside in mid-spring (March for most of the country). Cover the area you have planted with a cold frame for two to three weeks to allow the seedlings to establish themselves. Make sure the cold frame has air circulation and is not airtight, and make absolutely sure the plants do not dry out on sunny days, which can happen quickly in cold frames. Remove the cold frame once the plants are several inches tall and the soil is not in danger of freezing. You can also start cabbages indoors up to two months before the time you intend to transplant, but be aware that indoor cabbages will need full sunlight or artificial sunlight. Artificial sunlight must be kept within one inch of the top of the plants, and the plants can still easily get spindly and weak. Planting seed in a cold frame in spring is a much more reliable option.

Where to plant: Cabbages are not picky about soil. They will do well in clay or loamy soil.

How to plant: Space cabbages a couple of feet apart.

How to fertilize: Cabbages have deep taproots and don't generally need fertilizer. They can benefit from a dose of compost tea or the homemade fertilizer recipe in this book, applied just as the cabbage begins to form its head.

How to transplant: If you are using young transplants, harden them off for several days by setting them out into the sunlight for several hours (not a full day) and leaving them outside overnight. This allows the leaves of the plant to adjust to the shock of moving from indoor conditions to outdoor conditions. This shock can severely stunt or shock plants, especially if they have been grown in a greenhouse or under artificial lights. It is best to put the transplants into the garden on a cloudy day or just before a rainstorm. Transplants are watered on the same schedule as seeds, following this pattern: first day, plant and water. Second day, water again. Then skip a day of watering, water, skip two days, water, skip three days, until you are going ten days between waterings. Then water deeply, preferably overnight so the water soaks into the ground instead of evaporating in the sun.

When to harvest: After several hard frosts in autumn.

How to preserve: There are two ways to preserve cabbages—the "common" way and the Caleb way. The common way is to carefully pull up the entire cabbage, root and all, in late autumn and then "plant" the cabbage root in a bucket of damp sand and store the whole plant in a dark garage that doesn't freeze, cellar, or basement cold room for winter use. The Caleb way is lazier. Danish Ballhead cabbages are hardy and form tight heads. I simply leave the cabbages in the garden all winter and harvest each head as needed. About January we start to get temperatures as low as twenty degrees below zero during the night, and this will freeze the cabbage head solid. I find it in the deep snow, break off the head, bring it in the house, and use it immediately, and it is as good as fresh and better than a cabbage that has been stored in a cellar for months.

RECOMMENDED VARIETIES

- Danish Ballhead cabbage

Cantaloupe and Melons

Cucumis melo | Annual

I believe that no one—no one—in the world has grown as many varieties of cantaloupe as I have. I have grown more than three hundred varieties of cantaloupes. I have tested every single variety of heirloom cantaloupe available from every seed company in the United States and often Europe. I have grown the rarest cantaloupes in the world, thanks to Seed Savers Exchange. I have grown varieties that have been saved for generations in single families, never available to the public, not even through Seed Savers Exchange. Why did I raise all these varieties? Because they were so frustrating! Trying to find a variety of cantaloupe that is a superstar in a garden without black plastic has been the hard work of many years. But I have done it.

If you have read my Forgotten Skills books, seen a photo tour of my garden on my blog (check one out at http://calebwarnock.blogspot.com/2012/11/this-is-what-winter-gardening-looks.html), or if you are one of the thousands of people who have toured my garden in person (on class days only!), you know that I am passionate about just one single kind of cantaloupe—Noir des Carmes Cantaloupe. This rare variety is centuries old, said to be originally developed by the Carmelite monks of France. Bless those monks! The problem with growing cantaloupes today is that we have hybridized the heck out of these wonderful fruits, and those hybrid varieties are fragile and weak (not to mention they don't produce true seed), requiring an increasingly artificial environment to produce good crops. By *artificial*, I mean black plastic and petrochemical fertilizer. I have no interest in using either one because I focus on being self-reliant in my garden, and growing cantaloupes on black plastic with petroleum-based fertilizer is the opposite of self-reliance. I believe my garden should pay me in food instead of me paying for my garden. I am told I have to buy, buy, buy stuff from the nursery or hardware store to "make my garden work." Nonsense.

So what is so special about Noir des Carmes cantaloupes? They are an organic gardener's dream. They are a dream for no-till gardening. They are a dream for self-reliant gardeners. Believe it or not, this is both a winter and summer cantaloupe, traditionally grown in hot beds starting in January. (I have sprouted them in the first week of February in my geothermal greenhouse!) Noir des Carmes grows prolifically—tons of melons—without any black plastic. It is one of the very earliest melons to mature. And best of all, it turns from dark green to orange overnight when it is ripe, so you never have to guess! Noir des Carmes works well for fresh winter garden growing as well as summer. This is the best self-seeding cantaloupe on earth, as long as you don't let other cantaloupe pollinate it. And there is mounting evidence that this cantaloupe is self-pollinating, which is remarkable.

"Who cares about all of that?" you might say. "What really matters is flavor, so how is the flavor?" Perfect!

When to plant: Plant after all danger of frost in the outdoor garden. If growing Noir des Carmes in winter or spring, use a hot bed as outlined in my *Backyard Winter Gardening* book.

Where to plant: Noir des Carmes is not picky about soil and will do well in clay or loam.

How to plant: Plant seeds one inch deep, spaced about a foot apart.

How to fertilize: Noir des Carmes does not really need fertilizer if you have good soil, but it responds well to being watered with compost tea or the homemade fertilizer recipe in this book, if needed, once when young and once again just as the melons begin to form. Never fertilize a cantaloupe after the melons are larger than the size of an egg, because the fertilizer can cause a growth spurt, which will crack open the immature melons before they are ripe. Overwatering melons as they ripen can also cause them to crack open. By the time melons are ripening, you should be watering (deeply) only once every ten days. If there has been two inches of rain within the past ten days, or if the ground is moist, or if the weather is cooling down, do not water cantaloupes at all because you risk cracking the melons open just before they ripen.

How to transplant: Tests in my garden have repeatedly shown that, because of shock, melons that are transplanted do not produce melons any faster than melons that are direct seeded either in a hot bed or in the open garden after all danger of frost. I do not recommend transplanting melons.

When to harvest: Noir des Carmes cantaloupes literally turn from dark green to orange overnight when they are ripe. As soon as they change colors, they are ready to eat. They will not hold much longer than three days, so eat them quickly. Every single year at our house, there comes a moment when we are cantalouped-out. We've been eating fresh

Noir des Carmes Canteloupe

ripe cantaloupe every day, several times a day for a couple weeks and we just don't want anymore—yet the garden is still full of ripe cantaloupes because a single Noir des Carmes plant can produce eight to fifteen cantaloupes! At this point each year, I make Ambrosia Jam, which is simple. Mash together three cups of ripe cantaloupe and three cups of ripe peaches. Bake this in a glass casserole dish for sixty minutes, stirring every twenty minutes. Remove from the oven, cool, and eat fresh on homemade natural yeast bread, or freeze. To our family, this is the best jam in the world.

How to preserve: Ripe cantaloupe can be cut from the rind and frozen for later use in smoothies, baby food, or for making jam.

RECOMMENDED VARIETIES

- Noir des Carmes Cantaloupe

Carrots

Daucus Carota | Biennial

Simply put, this vegetable is essential. If your reason for gardening is flavor, you already know that you cannot find carrots in the grocery store that come close to the flavor of a fresh garden carrot. If your reason for gardening is self-reliance and cutting your grocery store bill, carrots are an integral part of home cooking. If you garden to create health for your family, carrots are necessary. If you garden to make green smoothies, carrots add an important boost of flavor, vitamins, and minerals.

Without experience, carrots can also be frustrating. Why? They are slow to sprout, quick to die for lack of water, sensitive to nitrogen and bad soil, and thwarted by rocks. Luckily the solutions, as outlined below, are simple.

When to plant: Plant as soon as the soil can be worked in spring. This is critical because carrots require a long, moist germination period with access to sunlight. Carrots are one of the few vegetables that benefit from sunlight to help them sprout.

Where to plant: Plant directly into garden soil. Carrots demand a foot of loamy soil free of rocks, with good drainage. Clay soil tends to stunt the growth of carrots and encourage disease related to lack of drainage. It is critical for the soil to have medium-to-low nitrogen content; otherwise the mature carrots will be covered in hair-like roots.

Autumn planting and greenhouse planting: Certain varieties of carrots will be harvestable in early winter when planted in late summer. These primarily include Scarlet Nantes, Danvers, and Paris Market. Plant them following the directions above, making sure they stay moist. Cover them with a cold frame before the ground freezes. I start harvesting them at Thanksgiving, when they are baby-carrot sized.

These also do well in a greenhouse for overwintering, as long as the soil in the greenhouse does not freeze. In a greenhouse, start them in late summer or early autumn and harvest them at any size. They are full-sized in March and April in my greenhouse. In this way, we have a self-sufficient carrot supply 365 days a year.

How to plant: Press the seed firmly into the top of the prepared soil. Water gently. Vigorous watering can dislodge the root, killing the seedling. For best germination, the seeds must be kept evenly moist. This is easiest to accomplish if you plant the seeds early in the season, as soon as the soil can be worked outside.

How to fertilize: Carrots do not like to be fertilized because extra nitrogen will make the roots hairy with small rootlets. If you are growing carrots in soil that has been enriched in compost, there is no need to fertilize them. If you are growing carrots in native soil, use the homemade organic backyard fertilizer recipe in this book because it will not be so high in nitrogen that it will cause hair roots on your carrots.

How to transplant: Carrots should not be transplanted because this creates stress to the taproot, which is what develops into the carrot you will eat.

When to harvest: You can begin harvesting baby carrots about fifty days after the carrots sprout, but keep in mind that every baby carrot you take is one less full-grown carrot you will be able to harvest later. Harvest carrots just before the ground freezes in early winter.

How to preserve: Carrots can be preserved in the ground by covering them with a foot-deep layer of hay or straw, which acts as a blanket to keep them from freezing. Allow snow to cover the hay or straw in winter, as this helps insulate the carrots. Dig them out on a sunny winter day once a month, bringing in a month's worth of carrots to put in your fridge. The downside of this method is that sometimes voles or other hungry critters will find them and "go shopping" in winter. Carrots can also be covered with autumn leaves or pine needles. Carrots can also be preserved by cutting all but an inch of the leaves off and then "planting" the root in a container of damp, clean sand. This container should be kept somewhere dark and cool for winter storage. A windowless garage that doesn't freeze in the winter is ideal, or a root cellar if you have one.

RECOMMENDED VARIETIES

- **Amarillo Carrot:** These big yellow beauties are among the earliest maturing of all carrots and have a beautiful light yellow color and a crisp, sweet, bright flavor that I love.
- **Caleb's Color Carrot Mix:** I like to grow and eat colorful food, so each year, I grow a mixture of carrots that includes purple, red, yellow, white and, yes, even some orange varieties. I select and blend this mixture myself.
- **Scarlet Nantes:** These are fast-growing orange carrots with a scarlet blush on top. These are slender carrots, not fat roots. They do well in spring and also when planted in autumn and are loved for their sweet flavor.
- **Danvers, also called Danvers Half Long:** These are shorter than most varieties and are called Half Long for this reason. These are traditional wedge-shaped carrots. They do well in poor soil because they are shorter, and they also produce faster. Great for both spring and fall planting.
- **Amsterdam Forcing:** These are perfect for autumn planting and green-house planting (and also do well as spring planted), but this seed is no longer available, and import laws make it difficult to bring in from Europe. I do my best to keep it in stock at SeedRenaissance.com since we are the only US seller.
- **Any heirloom variety:** I sell Snow White, Atomic Red, Lunar White, Cosmic Purple, and other heirloom colored carrots as part of the color mix package.

Cauliflower

Brassica oleracea | Biennial

When to plant: Most of the United States does not have a long enough growing season to start cauliflower directly from seed in the garden, despite the fact that cauliflower seed can be planted earlier than most vegetables. For success, use a short day-count cabbage like Snowball Cauliflower, and plant the seeds outside in mid-spring (March for most of the country). Cover the area you have planted with a cold frame or row cover until the plants have a good start. Permanently remove the frame or cover when most nights are consistently above freezing. Make sure the cold frame has air circulation and is not airtight, and make absolutely sure the plants do not dry out on sunny days, which can happen quickly in cold frames. You can also start cauliflower indoors up to two months before the time you intend to transplant, but be aware that indoor cauliflower will need full sunlight or artificial sunlight. Artificial sunlight must be kept within one inch of the top of the plants, or the plants can easily get spindly and weak. Planting seed in a cold frame in spring is a much more reliable option.

Where to plant: Cauliflower are not picky about soil. They will do well in clay or loamy soil.

How to plant: Space cauliflower twenty-four inches apart.

How to fertilize: Cauliflowers have deep taproots and don't generally need fertilizer.

How to transplant: If you are using transplants, harden them off for several days by setting them out into the sunlight for several hours (not a full day) and leaving them outside overnight. This allows the leaves of the plant to adjust to the shock of moving from indoor conditions to outdoor conditions. This shock can severely stunt or shock plants, especially if they have been grown in a greenhouse or under artificial lights. It is best to put the transplants into the garden on a cloudy day, or just before a rainstorm. Transplants are watered on the same schedule as seeds, following this pattern: first day, plant and water. Second day, water again. Then skip a day of watering, water, skip two day, water, skip three days, until you are going ten days between waterings. Then water deeply, at least two inches, preferably overnight so that the water soaks into the ground instead of evaporating in the sun.

When to harvest: Harvest as soon as the full, tight head develops. As soon as open spaces begin to appear in the "curd" of the cauliflower head, your head is starting to be past its prime and should be harvested immediately.

How to preserve: Wash, chop, and blanch in boiling water for ninety seconds, and freeze for storage.

RECOMMENDED VARIETIES

- Snowball cauliflower

Celery

Apium graveolens | Biennial

Water, water, water—that is what it takes to successfully grow celery. Like stevia, celery is a water-loving plant that is happier than most plants to have "wet feet," meaning wet soil. Celery appreciates humidity and tends to stunt and bolt in dry heat. However, this vegetable is essential in Italian cooking, giving slow-simmered tomato sauces part of their unique flavor characteristic. So while celery can be finicky to grow, the rewards are worth it. If you are living in a place where celery is easy to grow, count yourself among the lucky. Celery is more difficult to grow where I live, especially in a garden that only gets watered four times a year, as mine does. I grow celery in the greenhouse. But most of the time, I substitute the ribs of Swiss chard for any recipe that calls for celery. So if you live in a dry climate, as I do, chard is much easier to grow and far more drought tolerant. See the Swiss chard chapter of this book on page 153 for instructions.

When, how, and where to plant: Celery likes continual moisture without being in a puddle. The seeds can be slow to germinate, sometimes taking a month or more, especially if the water is too wet or if the soil dries out between watering. If the soil does become dry, you run the real risk that the seeds will never germinate. Dry soil will also quickly kill young seedlings.

In most areas of the country, celery is happy to be planted two times a year—in earliest spring in the greenhouse in a container with no drainage holes or in mid-summer outdoors in a container with no drainage holes or in swampy garden soil that will stay constantly moist, if you have access to such a thing. Whether planted indoors or outdoors, the seeds must remain constantly moist—if they dry out at all, it is likely that the seed will never germinate. They also need good access to sun from the day they sprout, so starting them in the house is difficult—they will need direct sun or artificial full-spectrum light. If you plant in the greenhouse, transplant outdoors after all danger of frost has passed, but beware that temperatures in the nineties or above can cause the plants to bolt, meaning they will produce tiny white flowers and seed instead of producing stalks. If you plant at the end of July, you will have a better chance of producing a crop of celery in autumn so that the plant is maturing just as the temperatures are becoming more balmy.

How to fertilize: Celery does not need fertilizer in good soil. Over-fertilizing celery can cause the plants to bolt to flower heads instead of producing stalks.

How to transplant: Transplant with lots of water. If transplanting from the greenhouse to the garden, make sure the plant never runs out of water. This is the same if you are transplanting from the garden to the greenhouse in autumn before the first frost of winter. Celery is easier to start from seed at the height of summer, and also easier to transplant into the greenhouse in fall, if you plant it in a container. Then you can just take the whole container into the greenhouse in autumn without ever having to disturb the roots.

When to harvest: Take off the outer stalks of the plant as needed, leaving the newest stalks in the center of the plant to continue growth.

How to preserve: Dry or freeze.

RECOMMENDED VARIETIES

- Calypso Celery and varieties listed at SeedRenaissance.com

Chinese Cabbage

Brassica rapa | Biennial

When to plant: Chinese cabbage prefers cool temperatures, and the seed will germinate in cool soil. Chinese cabbages do well in greenhouses, cold frames and row covers in winter as long as the ground is not allowed to freeze. When planting seeds in the open garden, plant in spring or autumn. Chinese cabbages are fast growing but may not form a tight head if your cool season is short. A loose-leaf head can be used like a tight head. Flowers and "rapini" (unopened flowers) are edible and delicious. In my geothermal winter greenhouse, Chinese cabbage begins to bloom in early February. I harvest the tips of the flower stalks to use in stir-fry. The tips have a flavor and texture like asparagus or broccoli stalks.

Where to plant: Chinese cabbage does well in most soil types, including clay, sand, and loam.

How to plant: Rake seeds lightly into soil, or plant in rows eight inches apart. Keep damp until germination, which can take one week or several weeks if soil is cool.

How to fertilize: Chinese cabbage will not need fertilizer if your soil is rich or amended with compost. Fertilizing can encourage the plants to bolt (produce seed stalks) instead of producing a head, especially in warm temperatures. If your soil is poor, you can apply compost tea or homemade fertilizer.

How to transplant: Chinese cabbages are easy to transplant, but transplanting is rarely necessary. In autumn and spring, they can be started indoors, in full light, and transplanted outdoors once they have germinated. In early spring, they will need a cold frame, cloche, or row cover to protect them once outside. Plants will withstand light frosts, and established plants may withstand one to two heavy frosts. Plants will not withstand prolonged direct contact with snow. Chinese cabbage should

not be transplanted in summer because this plant does not like heat and will likely quickly go to seed or die.

When to harvest: Harvest leaves at any size. For continual harvest, take only the outer leaves, and the leaves at the center will continue to grow out as long as the weather is not hot. If you have a long cool season, the plant will produce a head, which can be harvested whole.

How to preserve: Chinese cabbages are not generally preserved.

RECOMMENDED VARIETIES

- Chinese Cabbage Michihili

Collards

Brassica oleracea | Biennial

This leafy vegetable is extremely easy to grow and happily self-seeds. Collard leaves can become huge, but they taste best when they are young. The center rib of collard leaves may be used in place of broccoli or as a supplement to broccoli in some recipes. The leaves are shredded like cabbage, to be eaten on tacos or chopped to be cooked as greens. The raw leaves may be chopped as an ingredient in salad. Collards have one of the longest harvest windows in the garden. You can begin harvesting the tender leaves in spring. Harvest them through the summer and through autumn until the soil freezes solid. If you use a cloche or tall cold frame, you can harvest the leaves through most of winter too. The outer leaves are harvested, always leaving the center leaves.

When to plant: Once. This answer is not meant to be facetious. Collards are my favorite of all the brassica species for many reasons, not the least of which is that they are really the only brassica that easily self-perpetuates. Collards are easier to grow than broccoli, just because broccoli tends to have such a small harvest window before the plant bolts and the florets begin to lose their flavor and texture. Brussels sprouts are difficult to grow in most areas of the country mostly because they are often attacked by aphids before the sprouts can get to harvestable size. Cauliflower is difficult to blanch and has a small harvest window. Cabbage is a favorite of ours, but collards produce more food pound for pound. And collards have a better flavor than kohlrabi, which also has a much shorter harvest window. Collards, however, shine in the garden with their voluminous produce, huge harvest window, and great mild flavor—and best of all, they only need to be planted once. I planted a few collard seeds in my garden years ago and the plants have self-seeded every year since. I love nothing more than garden vegetables that do all the work for me. Collards also shine for one other simple reason—of all the brassicas, they have proven to be the most aphid-resistant in my garden. This may because the fettle greens and the collards are in flower in my garden at the same time (they do not cross), and the aphids prefer the fettle greens for whatever reason. If you want collards to plant themselves, be prepared to let them move. They move three to four feet every year in my garden, meaning that they may block a pathway for a year. I'm happy to give them a pathway since I can easily go around them, but if having them in a pathway is a problem in your garden, simply transplant them to where you want them in mid-spring.

Where to plant: In clay or loamy soil.

How to plant: Seeds should be planted a quarter-inch deep.

How to fertilize: No fertilizer necessary.

How to transplant: Transplant when they are young, between two and six inches tall. Plants that are too old or too young may die from transplant shock or root shock.

When to harvest: Harvest the leaves at any size.

How to preserve: Blanch, chop, and freeze.

RECOMMENDED VARIETIES

- Collard Vates, an old variety

Corn

(Includes Sweet Corn and Popcorn)

Zea mays | Annual

Modern corn is one of the most fragile and artificial vegetables in the world. As you begin to learn about the history of growing corn and saving corn seed, you begin to learn just how vulnerable this species is. Wild corn, which can still be found in Mexico, resembles a dwarf version of broom corn and does not have ears. Corn is perhaps the most malleable plant in the garden, and I encourage everyone to try to save corn seed so you can see firsthand how fragile the world's seed-stocks are. Because corn is wind pollinated and does not self-pollinate, saving pure corn seed was difficult before the invention of hybrid and then genetically modified corn. Today, it is increasingly looking like keeping pure heirloom corn seed might be impossible in the long term, which would be a huge loss of centuries of work. Imagine a world where there is no public domain corn seed left, a world where the only corn seed in existence is patented, corporate-owned, and genetically modified or hybrid so that it does not produce true seed. This could be true within five years. Why? Because corn is wind pollinated, so no one can control the spread of genetically modified and hybridized genes.

When to plant: After all danger of frost has passed.

Where to plant: Corn likes clay or loam soil with some clay. If you live in a high-wind area or if you tend to overwater your garden soil without at least some clay content, the corn may topple because it cannot get a strong enough purchase on the soil to withstand the wind.

How to plant: Plant seeds one inch deep. It is essential that corn be planted in blocks of at least one hundred plants, if not more. This means you plant a block ten plants wide and ten plants deep. This is necessary for two reasons. First, every single silk on the corn

produces one kernel, and each silk has to accept its own male pollen in order to be viable. Second, the pollen is carried only by wind and not by insects. If you have ever grown corn in your backyard that was missing kernels here and there, this is because the silk that would have formed that kernel was not able to find a male pollen. If you plant one hundred corn plants in a single row, the wind will be hard pressed to get male pollen to each of those plants. But if you plant corn in a block, you have a much greater chance of allowing pollen access to the majority of plants—however, you will still likely find some missing kernels on the outside plants. The larger your block, the better your pollination will be.

How to fertilize: Use compost tea or the homemade fertilizer recipe in this book when the corn is young (four to six inches tall) and every three to four weeks thereafter, with the last application when the corn ears have begun to form.

How to transplant: Corn does not like to be transplanted.

When to harvest: There is a small window during which corn is ripe but not starchy. If left too long in the garden, it will develop starch and begin to lose it sugar as it works to become seed. Fresh-picked corn also begins to go starchy in about twenty-four to forty-eight hours, once picked. Once the silks of the corn have begun to dry, check ears daily for ripeness and harvest when you can use them fairly immediately. In addition to being boiled, fresh corn is delicious roasted whole in the ears on the outdoor grill.

How to preserve: Corn can be frozen or canned. My great-grandmother Lexia Dastrup Warnock still practiced the pioneer preservation method when I was a child. She would cut the fresh corn off the ears from her garden and let it air-dry in the house. Once dry, she would store the kernels in glass jars, and then in winter she would boil the corn in fresh milk and cream from the family cow until it was tender. Delicious!

RECOMMENDED VARIETIES

- **Stowell's Evergreen Sweet Corn**: This is my favorite corn ever, and it's called "evergreen" for a reason. This is one of the oldest original sweet corn varieties in America, and it was always used by the homesteaders and pioneers to extend the season—it stays sweet on the stalk for weeks for extended fresh picking. If you want to use it for winter, there are two options for using this rare, unusual corn. As detailed in my first Forgotten Skills book, just before the first frost of fall, you can pull the entire stalk up—roots and all—and hang it upside down in your garage or cellar. Treated like this, the corn will stay sweet and ripe for four to eight weeks. This is not a rumor—I've tested it! The second way this corn used to be used was boiling. This corn can be cut when ripe, dried, stored, and then boiled in milk in winter until it is plump and tender again—I've also done this, and it tastes great. It tastes exactly like the boiled corn my great-grandmother used to serve at her dinner table. Very nostalgic for me. I love this corn and grow it every year. This is yellow corn.

- **Country Gentleman**: This white sweet corn is the heirloom variety that comes closest to the sugary flavor of the genetically modified corn that I am strongly opposed to and will not grow in my garden. Country Gentleman is packed with rows of small white juicy kernels that are tender and flavorful when cooked. Yum!

- **Golden Bantam Sweet Corn**: This yellow sweet corn has that old-fashioned true corn taste that is so often missing from the genetically modified corn today. If you were ever lucky enough to have fresh corn out of your great-grandmother's garden, this is what that corn tasted like (and it very well could be this corn that your great-grandmother was growing!)

Cucumber

Cucumis sativus | Annual

In Japan, where I lived for two years, the farmers would pick fresh cucumbers from the garden in the morning and put them in a sheltered place in the stream that irrigated the fields and then eat these as a treat—sweet, crisp, crunchy, and hydrating. Most people don't know that there are more cucumber varieties than just the green kind you grow to make pickles—not that there is anything wrong with the old standard.

When to plant: After all danger of frost has passed.

Where to plant: Cucumbers are not picky about their soil. They will do well in clay or loam.

How to plant: Plant the seeds a half-inch deep, 14–18 inches apart. To be honest, I usually plant them about 12 inches apart and just let them grow on top of each other.

How to fertilize: With cucumbers, the goal is a sweet and juicy fruit, not a fruit that is huge. For this reason, cucumbers should not be fertilized.

How to transplant: You can start plants indoors up to six weeks before the expected last frost date, but the plants go through at least three weeks of transplant shock. In my experience there is not much reason to start them early—the transplants produce cucumbers almost at the same time that the direct-from-seed plants do. Why bother with the hassle?

When to harvest: Harvest when they are young and tender. Keep an eye on your cucumbers—it is amazing how fast they go from one inch to four or six inches long. The longer they sit on the vine, the less tasty they will be. Pick immediately when ripe.

How to preserve: Refrigerator pickles can be made easily and with no special equipment.

There are dozens of recipes on the Internet for this.

RECOMMENDED VARIETIES

- **Marketmore**—My favorite pickling cucumber—green, straight, sweet, prolific. Fast growing. Plant directly in the garden after all danger of frost.
- **Poona Keera**—This is a sweet, never bitter yellow cucumber that is perfect for fresh eating and salads. You will love the flavor!

Edamame

(Soybeans)

Glycine max | Annual

E*damame* is simply a Japanese word that has been adopted for varieties of soybeans that are eaten fresh out of the green shell, meaning the green beans are removed from the pod and eaten fresh and raw as a snack or side dish. Edamame, or soybeans, are an excellent source of protein and nutrition.

When to plant: After all danger of frost has passed.

Where to plant: Soybeans prefer loamy soil.

How to plant: Plant seeds a half-inch deep and eight inches apart.

How to fertilize: Soybeans don't necessarily need fertilizer but will benefit from compost tea or the homemade fertilizer recipe in this book, applied just as the beans are beginning to form.

How to transplant: Soybeans should not be transplanted. They should be directly seeded in the garden.

When to harvest: Harvest when the bean pods are plump, full, and tender.

How to preserve: Freeze.

RECOMMENDED VARIETIES

Any heirloom variety.

Eggplant

Solanum melongena | Annual

When to plant: Eggplants can be started indoors six weeks before your last frost date, or directly planted outside. When direct planting, use short day-count varieties for best success. Eggplants do not withstand frost and should be planted outdoors only after all danger of frost has passed.

Where to plant: Eggplants tolerate a wide range of soils.

How to plant: Plant seeds a quarter-inch deep and ten to twelve inches apart. Keep moist to germination, which will take one to two weeks.

How to fertilize: Eggplants benefit from compost tea or an occasional dose of homemade fertilizer.

How to transplant: Transplant only after all danger of frost passes.

When to harvest: Eggplant fruits taste best when harvested at six inches or less in size. The fruits will grow larger if allowed to stay on the vine.

How to preserve: Eggplant can be blanched and frozen but does not generally preserve its flavor very well.

RECOMMENDED VARIETIES

See varieties available at SeedRenaissance.com.

Garlic

Allium sativum | Perennial

Garlic varieties are divided into hard-neck types and soft-neck types. Hard-neck garlic is grown in cold northern climates and forms a seed stalk. Soft-neck types are grown in mild climates.

There are two ways to propagate backyard garlic: the perennial method and the annual method.

Perennial Method: Plant the garlic in the fall and allow it to multiply for two years before beginning to harvest some of the bulbs. The method works particularly well with elephant garlic, which is not actually garlic but a member of the leek family. Elephant garlic is unlikely to need cover in the winter, even in the north, but will benefit from cover with a cloche, cold frame, or a foot-deep layer of hay, straw, or leaves. True garlic may need some kind of cover each winter. The bulbs should be covered, as described above, before the ground freezes for winter and removed as soon as the ground around the cover thaws in early spring. The bulbs should be harvested by leaving some part of the clove and roots in the ground, which is easier with elephant garlic. True garlic will be easier to harvest partially in the third year, when the bulbs are expanding.

Annual Method: Heads of true garlic and elephant garlic are broken into individual cloves for planting in the fall. These cloves multiply to produce heads of garlic in summer, and these heads are harvested when the garlic dries in the garden. The heads are broken up, and the best cloves are saved for planting again in the fall, while the rest are eaten.

When to plant: In northern climates, both elephant and true garlic are planted in autumn, generally in mid-October. In mild southern climates, garlics are planted anytime in winter.

Where to plant: Garlics prefer clay or loamy soil.

How to plant: True garlic is planted one to two inches deep in the soil and four to five inches apart. Elephant garlic is planted more deeply, four to five inches deep and seven to eight inches apart.

How to fertilize: Garlic can benefit from one dose of compost tea in early summer.

How to transplant: Garlic transplants easily. Garlic can be started in the greenhouse in autumn, overwintered in the greenhouse, and then moved to the open garden in spring. Most gardeners, however, simply plant garlic in the fall and allow it to overwinter in the open garden.

When to harvest: Harvest in early autumn of the second year when the foliage begins to die back.

How to preserve: Garlic is allowed to dry in the garden and is then brought into the house to cure in indirect sunlight for several days. Cured garlic can be stored anywhere in the kitchen.

RECOMMENDED VARIETIES

Any heirloom variety. There are differences in flavor in most varieties, some being hotter, some being milder, some being more intense in aroma and flavor. Elephant garlic is milder by nature and is generally not used medicinally.

Sunchokes

Sunchokes

(Jerusalem Artichokes or Sunroot)

Helianthus tuberosus | Perennial

This vegetable is kind of like a cross between a potato and a sunflower, believe it or not. The tuber roots are eaten in soups and stews and are prized because they are not starchy and are low on the glycemic scale. These roots are also prized because they are ready to harvest in February, making them an important "hunger gap" food for previous generations for whom self-reliance was a necessity. The plants grow eight feet tall and, in mid-autumn, bloom with yellow sunflowers that are about a third smaller than common wild sunflowers (sunchokes do not cross with garden or wild sunflowers). I should also mention that sunchokes have historically been called Jerusalem artichokes, but because they have nothing to do with Jerusalem and they are not at all related to artichokes, there has been a movement among gardeners to change the name to sunchokes to better reflect the nature of this vegetable.

When to plant: Sunchokes are planted as root tubers and not by seed. The roots should be planted in early spring.

Where to plant: As perennial plants, sunchokes are going to forever live wherever you plant them, so choose a spot with full sun where they can be a permanent part of the landscape. With access to regular water, sunchokes can become invasive, so you should consider planting them in a place where they can be contained. They can be planted in deep pots that are buried in the ground.

How to plant: Sunchoke roots like to be near the surface. Plant them in clay or loamy soil about an inch below the surface.

How to fertilize: Sunchokes don't need fertilizer.

How to transplant: If you wish to start a new sunchoke patch, plant several of the tubers in the new location as soon as the ground can be worked in the spring.

When to harvest: As soon as the ground can be worked in spring.

How to preserve: Sunchokes can be stored in a cool, dark place like a windowless garage, basement cold room, or cellar.

RECOMMENDED VARIETIES

There are no varieties.

Sunchoke flowers

Kale

Brassica oleracea | Biennial

If you are looking for a vegetable that is easy to grow and highly nutritious, you need look no further than kale. But let's be honest. The thing that has thrown kale into the spotlight in recent years is the popularity of green smoothies. Green smoothies are health in a cup when they are prepared correctly. *Smoothie* is the keyword; the drink must be prepared with the full natural fiber, including both water-soluble and water-insoluble fiber. Simply taking the juice from a vegetable and drinking it, removed from the fiber, spikes the glycemic index, which causes chronic inflammation and type 2 diabetes, both deadly conditions. To make a green smoothie correctly, blend the entire vegetable. If you are only juicing, you aren't acting in your body's best interest.

Kale is one of the rare vegetables that gives two harvests a year—once in the spring and again in the fall. Kale is not a true perennial but a Dwarf Blue Siberian Kale—which does not cross with regular brassicas—and self-seeds reliably, making it perennial in my garden for all practical purposes.

When to plant: In spring.

Where to plant: In clay or loamy soil.

How to plant: Plant a quarter-inch deep and twelve inches apart.

How to fertilize: Not necessary.

How to transplant: Kale can be best planted when immature at two to five inches tall.

When to harvest: Leaves can be harvested at any time.

How to preserve: Freeze.

RECOMMENDED VARIETIES

- **Dwarf Blue Siberian Kale:** This variety does not cross with traditional kale or brassicas and is self-seeding, making it ideal for perennial garden.

Leeks

Allium ampeloprasum | (Includes Elephant Garlic)
Annual as Leeks, Perennial as Elephant Garlic

Leeks are easy to grow if you are easygoing about the harvest. What I mean is do not expect your garden leeks to look like grocery store leeks unless you want to put extra work into them. Grocery store leeks have been "blanched" by covering about eight inches of the stalk with soil. You can do this in the backyard garden by building a cardboard or wooden frame around the leek patch and filling it with compost that is pressed down and compressed until it is eight inches deep. Or you can grow leeks the lazy way, which I admit is the method I use most often: just let them grow. You will get a smaller leek, and you will need to use two to three leeks in place of one grocery store leek in your recipe. Leeks easily self-seed. I grow and sell Belgium Breeder's Winter Mix Leeks.

When to plant: In early spring, as soon as the ground can be worked.

Where to plant: In clay or loam.

How to plant: Plant seeds a half-inch deep and keep moist until germination. Plant six to twelve inches apart.

How to fertilize: Leeks benefit from two applications of compost tea: one application when the plants are six to eight inches tall and one when the plants are eighteen inches tall.

How to transplant: Leeks can be transplanted when they are two to six inches tall.

When to harvest: Anytime in autumn.

How to preserve: Can be dried, frozen, or allowed to stay in the garden until the ground freezes. Can be pulled up whole with the roots and stored in damp sand in a garage, basement cold room, or cellar.

RECOMMENDED VARIETIES

- Belgian Breeder's Winter Mix
- American Flag

Lettuce

Lactuca sativa | Annual

When to plant: Seed can be planted anytime beginning in early spring and ending in early fall. Many growers sow seeds every couple of weeks throughout spring for a succession of fresh lettuce. Winter varieties can be planted using the directions and varieties recommended in my *Backyard Winter Gardening* book.

Where to plant: Lettuce is happy in most soils, including clay, loam, and sand.

How to plant: Scratch the seeds lightly into the soil and keep moist until germination. The warmer the soil is, the faster the seeds will germinate. Seeds planted in July will germinate in about three days. Seeds planted in early spring might take several weeks to germinate.

How to fertilize: Not necessary, but they can be given an application of compost tea when young, between two to three inches tall.

How to transplant: Lettuce does not love to be transplanted, but if you need to transplant it, water the soil until it is muddy, and remove the plant from the muddy soil and transplant it into very wet, muddy soil. Muddy soil helps the roots to acclimatize more easily after being transplanted.

When to harvest: The outer leaves of any variety of lettuce can be harvested at any stage. Head lettuces can be harder to grow than leaf lettuce, depending on where you live. Head lettuce like humidity and need cooler temperatures for heads to form.

How to preserve: Lettuce is not preserved.

RECOMMENDED VARIETIES

- **Buttercrunch Lettuce:** This is my favorite perennial lettuce, as detailed in my Forgotten

Winter density lettuce

Skills books. In my garden, this lettuce comes back year after year if grown on ground you don't till. It is not a true perennial, but it self-seeds extremely reliably if you don't eat it all and let a few heads go to seed. It is dwarf-sized, with green leaves, and is one of the first to self-seed in spring, usually in late April or early May. It grows fast and works well for fresh winter garden growing as well as summer. A reliable self-seeder!

Caleb's Deep Winter Lettuce: Winner! All seed of this variety is taken only from plants that spent the winter in my backyard garden without any protection, despite minus nineteen below zero temperatures! I planted ten federal seed bank accession varieties on October 1 and grew them all winter without any cover or frame—and this variety was the clear winner! I am the only person in the world to offer this seed for sale, and because I developed the seed, I got to name it. It works well for fresh winter garden growing as well as summer.

Gabriella Lettuce: An amazing deep wine red lettuce that is a must-have for gourmet salads. Great taste, loose-leaf bunching lettuce. This lettuce is dark, dark red from the day it comes out of the ground and never changes color. Even better, it was the last lettuce to bolt in my garden, lasting midway through the heat of July. It's a new favorite of mine. It works well for fresh winter garden growing as well as summer.

Grand Rapids Lettuce: This is the all-time fastest-growing lettuce in all seasons of more than one hundred varieties of lettuce I have trialed! This stuff grows amazingly fast in fall and spring and even (astonishingly) grows a staggering four inches a week in February in a hotbed! This winter lettuce was the winner of a 1899 winter garden lettuce trial done by the Extension service. The leaves are delicate

Buttercrunch Lettuce

and not crunchy, and the flavor is mild. I will never be without this lettuce. If I'm running low on lettuce (we are self-sufficient on lettuce, meaning we grow all we eat), this is the lettuce I plant first. This lettuce came about in 1880, when Eugene Davis of Grand Rapids, Michigan, noticed that some variants of an ancient French winter lettuce called Curled Silesia were doing better than all others during winter. Mr. Davis saved seed from the best winter plants until other gardeners began to ask him for the seed. According to an article in the April 1, 1906, edition of *Gardening* magazine, this lettuce "was so well adapted for winter forcing (in cold frames and hot beds) that it came to be almost exclusively used by Grand Rapids gardeners and growers in other cities came to ask for 'that Grand Rapids lettuce' and seedsmen were obliged to add it to their lists."

I love this lettuce and its history. This lettuce is rarely grown today. That will change if I have my way! It works well for fresh winter garden growing as well as summer.

- **Green Oak Leaf Lettuce:** This is a frilly green lettuce that is extremely hardy—grows outside in my winter garden without any protection but grows three times faster in a cold frame. Gorgeous lettuce that is a must-have for gourmet salad mixes, with a fine flavor. This lettuce works well for fresh winter garden growing as well as summer.

- **Marvel of Four Seasons Lettuce:** This is a favorite of ours because of its stunning color—a red/bronze/green with touches of purple. The lettuce also has a better taste than most lettuces—and best of all, it grows well during all four seasons (cold frame in winter). Works well for fresh winter garden growing as well as summer. A reliable self-seeder.

- **North Pole Lettuce:** I am the only seller of this lettuce in the United States. This is a winner of my winter greenhouse lettuce trials. It was originally bred a century ago by the famous Fridtjof Nansen of Norway, who was awarded the Nobel Prize for peace in 1922. He is famous for pioneering exploration of the North Pole and also for his global work to stop starvation during and after the first World War. For more information about him, see the second chapter of my new *More Forgotten Skills* book.

- **Tom Thumb Lettuce:** This is actually an old French heirloom lettuce that was used for winter growing for hundreds of years. In my 2013 geothermal greenhouse trial of twenty lettuce varieties, this lettuce came in second place, sprouting from seed in the first week of January—you read that right—during a very snowy, bitter cold week when the high temperature in the greenhouse was thirty-four degrees and the low was twenty-eight degrees. (There is no artificial heat or electricity in my geothermal greenhouse.) This lettuce does well outside in cold frames during the winter (down to minus-seven below zero in my garden) and also grows very well outside in the spring and fall. Beautiful, round green loose-leaf heads. This is a dwarf size and is also cut-and-come-again, meaning you can cut it at ground level and it will grow back several times.

Marvel of Four Seasons Lettuce

- **Winter Density Lettuce:** Winter Density Lettuce is a very old winter lettuce that has been used in winter gardens for hundreds of years. It performs excellently in my winter cold frames! This is a green leaf lettuce with a slightly sweet flavor. It works well for fresh winter garden growing as well as summer.

- **Winter Green Jewel Romaine:** This is the very best of all winter lettuces and is the lettuce I grow the most on my property year-round. I love the crunch and taste, and I love that you can plant this lettuce thickly and close together in huge amounts out of it. Best of all, cut this lettuce at the soil level and it grows back again and again! It will stay unprotected in the garden into December and does well in winter cold frames. It is both cold hardy and heat resistant! This lettuce is sold by no one else in the world! It works well for fresh winter garden growing as well as summer.

Mangels

(Fodder beets)

Beta vulgaris | Biennial

After becoming almost completely extinct, there has been a small resurgence of interest in mangels. Mangels are a type of field beet that have been grown throughout the centuries as feed for horses, cows, oxen, donkeys and other livestock. Because they are a source of protein, are easy to store in winter, and grow large, mangels were one of the most important sources of winter food for farmers who kept livestock overwinter before the invention of modern baled hay or agricultural stores selling bags of winter livestock feed. Overwintering a livestock animal in previous centuries was a very different enterprise than it is today. Historically, overwintering was done self-reliantly, meaning the farmer had to grow in summer all the food the animals would need once the ground was frozen. The way animals are fed over winter today would have been considered luxurious or even wasteful in days gone by. In those days, the goal was to keep the animals alive through winter. It was considered normal for animals to lose weight in winter and fatten in summer as preparation for winter. Mangels cannot match the protein content of modern winter feeds but are still useful for anyone on small acreage who is trying to feed livestock as self-sufficiently as possible. Mangels are grown exactly like beets but are harvested for human use only in the smallest stages. Mangels quickly grow quite large and woody and are inedible to the human palate after the early stages of growth. It is not unusual for a single mangel beet to weigh twenty pounds or more, especially when grown in composted manure. Mangel seed is rare today. Few varieties remain, mostly because the number of farmers who use mangels as feed has dwindled to nearly zero. Today there are a few small farms and homesteads that grow mangels at least as feed supplements for livestock, and there has been a small increase in the number of people looking for mangel seed. Mangel seed is available at SeedRenaissance.com.

Mustard Greens

Brassica juncea | Annual

This includes Osaka Purple Mustard greens, Sawtooth Mustard greens, Green Wave Mustard greens, and more.

When to plant: Spring, early summer, autumn.

Where to plant: Mustard greens are tolerant of most soil types.

How to plant: Rake seed lightly into soil. Keep moist to germination. Mustard greens like cool temperatures and will germinate in cool soil. Mustard greens will withstand light frosts.

How to fertilize: Mustard greens do not need fertilizer.

How to transplant: Mustard greens can be started indoors and transplanted in their early stages, but transplanting any plant causes shock. For this reason, mustard greens are best sown in a greenhouse or directly outside in a cold frame, cloche, or row cover.

When to harvest: Harvest the greens at any size. Take only the outer leaves for a continual harvest, or take the whole head.

How to preserve: Mustard greens are not generally preserved.

RECOMMENDED VARIETIES

- **Osaka Purple Mustard Greens:** These have a spicy-hot horseradish flavor and a beautiful purple color. They are reliable self-seeders and sprout both in early spring and early fall. They do well in winter greenhouses, cold frames, cloches, and row covers.

Onions

Allium cepa | Annual

There are many different types of onions grown by gardeners. Some produce flowers and seed, and some do not. Some are started from seed, and some are propagated by bulbs. Some are propagated by bulbils, and some are propagated by seeds and bulbs.

When to plant: Onion seeds can be planted in late autumn for spring germination, early spring as soon as the ground can be worked, or anytime in spring while the soil is still cool. Onion seeds will not do well if planted in warm summer weather. Onion seeds are generally planted thickly in a small space. When they sprout, they look somewhat like grass, with each seed producing a single green stem that is a thin tube. These sprouts are called "onion threads," and when they are two to three inches tall, they can be gently dislodged from the soil and transplanted. They will likely suffer from transplant shock, especially if the threads have been started indoors or in a greenhouse. However, so long as the ground does not freeze, the threads will produce plants even if they die back completely after being transplanted. The root will continue to live and produce new shoots. If the ground freezes, the root will die. Onion threads are spaced about five inches apart and buried only about a half-inch in the ground. Over time, a second stem will emerge, and so on. Growth of onion plants is slow in the beginning.

Onions that are planted from seed are divided into three categories: long-day onions, short-day onions, and day-neutral onions (also called intermediate-day onions). This day length refers to the number of hours of sunlight the plant must have on a summer day in order for it to produce a bulb. Short-day onions begin to form bulbs as soon as there are ten hours of summer sun. Long-day onions do not produce bulbs until there are 14 hours of summer sun in a day. Long-day

Green Mountain Huge Multiplier Onions

onions are grown in the north, in areas zone 6 and lower. Short-day onions are grown in the south, in garden zones 7 and higher. Day-neutral onions will form a bulb whether the sunlight is long or short. Day-neutral onions work best in zones 5 and 6. A long-day onion planted in a short-day zone will never produce a bulb. A short-day onion planted in a long-day zone may go to seed before producing a bulb. Wherever you live, it is important to plant the correct variety of onions for your area. For true seed, allow only one variety of onion to flower at a time. If other varieties in your garden begin to produce flower heads, cut them off to maintain varietal purity.

When to plant: Onions that produce bulbs instead of seeds are called potato onions, or multiplier onions. These onions are planted as one seed bulb, and that bulb divides into many bulbs over the summer and fall. In autumn, this clump of bulbs is harvested. The largest onions are kept for replanting. The rest are harvested for eating. Onion bulbs can be planted in autumn or spring. Bulbs smaller than 1½ inches in diameter overwinter best. Larger bulbs may need some protection, like a cold frame or row cover. They may also be overwintered under a layer of straw eight to twelve inches thick. Bulbs may also be harvested, dried outdoors for one to two days, and then stored indoors over winter in a cool dark place in a burlap bag or a bag made of some other breathable material. Onions should never be stored in closed containers or plastic, because even a small buildup of humidity will cause them to sprout roots and then rot. Potato (multiplier) onions can sometimes produce flower stalks and seeds. This will result in much smaller bulbs, and the bulbs may not store through winter. Because flowering is not a trait you want to encourage in multiplier onions, clip off any flowerheads that appear.

When to plant Walking or Topset onions: A few rare varieties of onions produce bulbils. These are called Egyptian Walking Onions or

Topset onions. These plants produce onions both at the roots and on top of the plants. The onions at the root will be the largest. The onions on top will be bulbils, and will be the largest in the first year. These topset onions will get smaller and smaller each succeeding year if the root bulbs are not transplanted or disturbed. This type of onion can be propagated from either root bulbs or topset bulbs. The bulbils can be harvested in summer or fall, stored indoors over winter, and planted in the spring or planted directly in the soil in autumn. These onions are perennial and extremely cold tolerant. The bulbs and bulbils should be planted so the top third of the bulb is uncovered.

These perennial onions are called Walking Onions because they do, in fact, walk, planting themselves as they go. They "walk" by producing bulbils at the top of the plant on stalks. In late summer or early autumn, these thick green stalks dry up, turn brown, and collapse. The weight of the bulbils tips the collapsed stalks to the ground, and the onions plant themselves by growing roots wherever they touch the ground. The bulbils are used in the kitchen as shallot-type onions and were historically prized because they are perennial and will outlive their owners in most cases. Walking onions may occasionally produce flowers, but these flowers, rare themselves, almost never produce true seed. These flowers can cross with other flowering onions in your garden. To prevent crossing, simply remove any flowers that might appear on walking onions.

Where to plant: Onions tolerate a wide range of soils but prefer clay and loam over sandy soil.

How to plant: Lightly rake seeds into the soil and keep moist to germination, which make take two weeks or several weeks in cold soil. Onions seeds are usually sown in a small space.

How to fertilize: In good soil, onions don't need much fertilizer. Onions can benefit from compost tea or homemade fertilizer once when they are young and once when they begin to form bulbs.

How to transplant: Onions, whether from seeds or bulbs, can be transplanted when young by carefully dislodging the roots from the soil without damaging the roots and replanting in a new spot.

When to harvest: Harvest onions when the green stem-leaves die back in autumn. For best eating, onions must be harvested before the ground freezes.

How to preserve: Onions from the garden should be trimmed of their leafy stalks and allowed to dry out of direct sunlight for one to two days in open air. After drying, gather the onions into a cloth sack and store in a cool, dry, dark place. Onions that sprout should be used immediately.

RECOMMENDED VARIETIES

- **Egyptian Walking Onions** (sold seasonally)
- **Shallot-type Multiplier Onions** (sold seasonally)
- **Green Mountain Huge Multiplier Onions** are by far the largest multiplier onions I've ever grown—some of these are the size of softballs. Five bulbs yielded a staggering fifty-five onions in my garden—and every one of them was larger than any other multiplier I've ever grown. Once you have these onions, you never have to buy them again—they multiply each year. This amazing onion was developed over a decade by the wonderful Kelly Winterton. This is a must-have onion for families looking to be self-sufficient. I sell them as seeds. To turn these seeds into bulbs, plant them in early spring in a greenhouse and move them outside as soon as the soil can be worked, or plant the seed outside as soon as the soil can be worked. At the end of summer, after the onions have died back, choose the largest bulbs for multiplying. I plant the bulbs in the fall (late September or early October) and cover them with a cold frame if temperatures are bitter. This method grows the largest onions, but you can also choose your largest bulbs in the fall, harvest them, store overwinter, and then plant in spring. Because this is landrace seed, you will get onions that are green, red, yellow, and white. Once you have bulbs to grow out, they will come true to color. Always keep your largest bulbs for multiplying the next season. Onion seed generally has a life of one to two years, so plant these seeds within one year.
- **Yellow Spanish Onions** are my favorite seed-producing storage onions. The flavor is great, and these onions store for months. They are easy to grow and easy to collect seed from.
- **Walla-Walla Onions** are a favorite onion for many people when it comes to flavor, but keep in mind that Walla-Wallas are not storage onions and will not store through winter.

Orach

(Mountain Spinach, French Spinach, Sea Purslane, or Salt Bush)

Atriplex hortensis | Annual

A cousin of spinach and used exactly like spinach, this beautiful red leafy vegetable brings nice color to the winter table and is full of nutrition too. Works well for fresh winter garden growing as well as summer.

When to plant: Orach self-plants easily, and if you have a no-till garden, you will likely only need to plant it once and you will have it the rest of your life. Orach can be planted in autumn for spring germination or in early spring.

Where to plant: Orach tolerates a wide range of soils.

How to plant: Press seed to soil or lightly rake into soil. Keep moist until germination. Thin to five inches apart.

How to fertilize: Orach does not need fertilizer and does well even in weak soil.

How to transplant: Orach does not need to be transplanted. Orach germinates well in cool soil and can be planted directly outside.

When to harvest: Harvest the leaves at any size.

How to preserve: Orach is not preserved.

RECOMMENDED VARIETIES

- Vernal Red Orach

Parsnip

Pastinaca sativa | Biennial

Parsnips are sort of a white version of carrots with a more earthy flavor and a less dense, slightly fibrous texture. These roots are easily mistaken for white carrots once they are peeled and sliced, but the leafy part of the plant looks more like parsley than carrots. Parsnips are savory, where carrots are sweet, making parsnips great for roasted dishes and slow-cooker dishes.

When to plant: Parsnips can be planted in early spring, and they do great in the greenhouses. Parsnips like to germinate in cold soil. They need a long growing season to mature and need frost to sweeten them for eating.

Where to plant: Plant in loamy soil with full sun exposure.

How to plant: Barely cover with soil. Keep moist. Don't be alarmed if germination is spotty—germination rates naturally vary with parsnips. Also don't be surprised if half or more of your seed never germinates. This is normal for parsnips.

How to fertilize: Use one or two applications of compost tea when the roots begin to develop (when the tops are about four inches tall) or use the homemade fertilizer recipe in this book.

How to transplant: Do not transplant.

When to harvest: Harvest in late fall, just before the ground freezes. Parsnips need several frosts to make the roots sweet for eating.

How to preserve: Parsnips can be left in the ground all winter if they are covered with about twelve inches of straw, hay, or leaves to act as a blanket to keep the ground from freezing in northern climates. Parsnip roots are very hardy.

RECOMMENDED VARIETIES

All heirloom varieties are worthy of the garden and taste great. Hollow Crown is a favorite of mine.

Peas

Pisum sativum | Vigna Unguiculata

I've never met anyone who doesn't love garden peas, and most gardeners want to extend their pea harvest to be as early and late as possible. Fresh peas are a treat. In this section, I've included a broad selection of different species that are sometimes called peas even when they are not common garden peas. All of these different species can be grown in the garden without fear of crossing.

When to plant: Peas should be planted as soon as the soil can be worked in spring. Peas may be planted in late autumn before the ground freezes, but there is a larger risk that the seeds will be eaten by predators or succumb to rot.

Where to plant: Peas do well in loamy or clay soil in full sun or partial sun areas. If planted in late spring or early summer, peas can be planted in light shade.

How to plant: Plant one inch deep and four to five inches apart.

How to fertilize: Peas don't require fertilizer. In my experience, peas that have been fertilized seem to go starchy faster.

How to transplant: There is no advantage to transplanting peas, so peas should be sown directly in soil.

When to harvest: Peas should be harvested every two to three days once the pods begin to ripen. This will allow the most peas to be harvested at maximum flavor. Peas left on the vine can become starchy within a week, depending on the variety.

How to preserve: Peas are best preserved by blanching and freezing. Canning peas is possible but negatively affects the flavor. Snow peas also can be blanched and frozen.

RECOMMENDED VARIETIES

- **Cascadia Peas:** This variety of pea withstands several hard frosts and is extra early. It is truly prolific, with large peas and the largest harvest compared with other varieties I tested. It has a traditional garden pea flavor and large bushy plants.

- **Golden Sweet Snow Peas:** This is an extra early variety. Can be harvested as Snow Peas or regular peas. Not as prolific as Cascadia but still produces a good harvest. The snow peas are a beautiful pale florescent green. Plants can grow to four feet tall or more.

- **Tom Thumb Peas:** This variety produces peas a week earlier, at least, of all other pea varieties (and I have tested hundreds of varieties). It does this by making a small plant, and each plant produces only a handful of peas. These are great for early food but will not provide a huge harvest.

- **Sugar Ann:** Another early variety that is prolific and has a great sweet flavor.

Cascadia Peas

Peppers

(Includes Sweet Peppers and Chili Peppers)

Capsicum annuum | Annual

Some people are passionate about garden peppers, with strong opinions about flavor, variety, color, and heat. Peppers are fairly easy to grow as transplants but can sometimes be difficult to germinate.

When to plant: Plant after all danger of frost has passed. Some gardeners find it preferable to start peppers indoors about four weeks before the expected last frost date, however pepper plants require full sun or full-spectrum artificial light.

Where to plant: In clay or loamy soil in full-sun areas. After they are established, peppers prefer hot, dry weather. If you live in an area with humidity, consult your local expert gardeners for varieties that work best in your area.

How to plant: Cover seed with a quarter-inch of soil and keep moist until germination, which will take about a week.

How to fertilize: Whether or not peppers benefit from fertilizer is debated among gardeners. Fertilizer can make the fruit seem artificially large, and some people think this affects the flavor, while others do not. My recommendation is one application of compost tea or the homemade fertilizer recipe in this book just as the fruits begin to form.

How to transplant: Harden off the plants and plant outside after all danger of frost has passed.

When to harvest: Some varieties may indicate ripeness by changing color, while others do not change color. Pick when the fruit is large and perfect.

How to preserve: Peppers may be air dried or machine-dehydrated. Dehydrated peppers may be preserved whole, sliced, or ground to powder. Peppers can also be canned or frozen.

RECOMMENDED VARIETIES

Seeds for medicinal cayenne are available on SeedRenaissance.com. There are hundreds of varieties of peppers, and afficiandos have strong preferences in garden chili and sweet pepper varieties. Some varieties should be harvested with care because even touching the skin of the pepper can transfer the oil from the pepper onto the gardener's hands, which can then be transferred to the eyes or to children, causing pain.

Potatoes

Solanum tuberosum | Annual

Gardeners tend to grow potatoes for one of two reasons: for the flavor of new potatoes or for mature potatoes for self-reliance. Most gardeners will likely need to choose one or the other unless they have a lot of room to grow potatoes and can grow enough for both needs. If you have never tasted truly new potatoes, you are in for a treat—they taste nothing like the starchy potatoes from the store or a cellar. New potatoes are harvested relatively early in the season. However, every new potato you harvest costs you a full-grown potato that you could have had later in the season. I tend to indulge in one or two harvests of new potatoes each year just for the flavor, while allowing the majority of my potatoes to mature to their large size for winter eating.

The size of your mature potatoes is going to depend entirely on the variety of potato you are growing and the amount of fertilizer you use. Potatoes are one of the garden vegetables that visibly and noticeably benefit from fertilizer and are happy to have a dose of compost tea as often as every two weeks. The diversity of size, color, and flavor among potatoes is staggering. Some large potatoes lack in flavor and nutrition compared to, for example, a purple thumb-type of potato, which is purple all the way through and full of vitamins and nutrition but will never produce a huge potato. Sadly, the variety of commercially available seed potatoes is very limited, and the kinds of potatoes available for purchase in stores is extremely limited, so for anyone who wants to experience even a fraction of what potatoes have to offer, growing your own is the only option. You could easily grow a handful of potato varieties a year and never grow the same variety twice in your life.

When to plant: Potatoes are tricky because they like cold soil and cool temperatures, but they are also frost sensitive. This year, as with most years, I planted potatoes in April, some in beds of compost and some in beds of straw. Potatoes planted in straw are always slower to emerge because they must grow up through a foot of straw, making the plants nearly full grown when they finally see the light of day. Potatoes growing in compost come up faster. A hard frost in early May killed all of my compost potatoes; luckily my straw potatoes had not emerged from the top of the straw yet and were untouched by the freeze. The compost potatoes did grow back, but it remains to be seen whether the potatoes I harvest will be stunted because of the setback. I tell this story because it illustrates some of the potential challenges with potatoes—plant them too early and they will be frost-killed. Plant them too late and they will never produce a large potato harvest because they struggle in the heat.

Mountain Rose Potatoes

Additionally, potatoes can be extremely susceptible to disease, both during the growing season and transferring from the seed potatoes to the next crop. Clay soil strongly promotes disease in potatoes. Over-watering promotes disease, and underwatering stunts potato growth. Some people swear by growing potatoes in sand, but the problem with sand is the potential for salt contamination. Unwashed sand can be cheap but might contain naturally occurring salt or alkali, which will cause the potatoes to be stunted or never sprout. Washed sand can still contain salt and can be expensive. I find compost or straw to be the two best options for most backyard gardeners.

Straw Method: Choose a clear space in the garden. Lay seed potatoes out in a grid, roughly five inches apart. I recognize that this is much closer than most garden books recommend, but for heirloom potatoes, this is usually the best spacing because most heirlooms produce medium-sized potatoes. Then cover the seed potatoes with a blanket of twelve inches of loose straw or hay. Leaves should not be used because they form a mat and smother the seed potatoes. Pine needles can be used, but they will not be fully decomposed by the end of the growing season, so you will need to harvest the potatoes with spade or garden fork and not with your hands or you will get poked (trust me, I'm speaking from experience). However, potatoes have a special affinity for pine needles because the needles are so strongly acidic, so you may want to consider at least a partial layer of pine needles if you have access to them. If you are using straw or hay, you may use old straw or hay, or straw harvested from your own garden if you grow your own wheat or oats or barley, as we do at our house. (I recognize almost no one does this, but growing your own wheat is easy!) Water them once a week until the potatoes sprout. Notice that there is no soil covering or digging involved with this method—you simply put the potatoes on the ground and cover them. Potatoes only grow up, they never grow down, so wherever you put the seed potato, the plant will grow up from there, and the new potatoes will form around and above the seed potato. I have been growing and teaching this method for years now, and I like to tell people this in my classes: At some point, you will get mad at me and will be tempted to want to cuss me out, saying, "That darn Caleb! He told me to plant my potatoes in straw. I planted them six weeks ago, and nothing! My potato crop is a failure, and it is Caleb's fault!" I've gotten emails like this, and I always reply and say, "Wait and be patient. Your potatoes will emerge, fully grown in another week or two." You have to remember with the straw potato method that the potato plant has to vine up through those twelve inches of straw before it emerges from the straw.

Once the green shoots of the potato plants have emerged, the plants will suddenly be larger than plants from potatoes planted the same day in the same garden in compost or in the traditional soil. Planting in straw also has the important benefit of really cutting down on disease in potatoes. Most potato diseases are encouraged by poor drainage. When you use the straw method, the water is absorbed by the straw, and any excess simply drains away, so poor drainage is never an issue (unless you live in an area prone to rain, in which case you would plant the potatoes on top of a raised bed and then cover them with straw so that the potatoes are never in standing water). You might think that growing the straw method would leave the potatoes without any fertilizer, but the straw at the bottom begins to decompose as the garden season goes on, providing some nutrients. However, potatoes grown in straw will produce the best crop if you apply compost tea as much as every two weeks, or if you sprinkle a generous helping of blood and bone meal on the ground and over the first couple of inches of straw. Blood meal and bone meal is the ideal organic fertilizer and is exactly what it sounds like—dried, powdered blood and crushed, powdered bone. Blood and bone meal is sold in garden stores, hardware stores, and nurseries nationwide. If you want to know how to make self-reliant blood and bone meal, read the chapter of my *More Forgotten Skills* book titled "So You Want to Live Green? Kill a Rooster."

When using the straw method, you can plant the seed potatoes inside a twelve-inch-tall grow-box to contain the straw, or you can simply do as a friend of mine does—lay the seed potatoes out on the ground wherever there is room and lay the straw over them in a pile with no box or container at all. Either way works well. Thousands of people have toured my garden (by appointment only!), and one of the most frequent questions I get is this: "Doesn't the straw blow everywhere in the wind?" The honest answer is no. Loose straw is kind of like a ball of string, especially after it has been watered once or twice. We have ferocious, prolonged windstorms of up to ninety miles per hour where I live and a phenomenon each fall called "microburst storms" which are essentially mini tornadoes. I have never, not even once, had a problem with the straw blowing out of my potato beds. (I do contain my straw potatoes in a foot-tall box of untreated pine.)

Compost Method: Potatoes that are grown in raised beds in pure compost will produce a harvest that is 30 percent to 50 percent larger than straw-grown potatoes by weight. (I have tested this). However, the downside is that you will need a large volume of compost if you are growing more than a handful of plants, which most gardeners are. If you are buying compost, the increased yield is not offset by the enormous cost. Creating enough compost in your backyard can be difficult using traditional methods, and impossible if you are trying to use a store-bought composting device, which will only yield a small volume of compost a year. You can easily grow a huge amount of compost using my grow-posting method, which will be discussed in another book. Meanwhile, if you can produce a volume of self-sufficient

RECOMMENDED VARIETIES

- Mountain Rose is my all-time favorite variety of potato.

free compost, I suggest you use the compost method simply because you will get more and larger potatoes. To use the compost method, lay out your potatoes in a grid with five inches between seed potatoes, and then cover with eight to twelve inches of compost. Do not use mulch. Do not use fertilizer.

Where to plant: Potatoes prefer light soil that is a balance of sand and loam. Few areas in the country have ideal soil for growing potatoes, and this is why the French, centuries ago, developed the straw growing method.

How to plant: Potatoes should ideally be planted twelve inches deep or deeper.

How to fertilize: Potatoes can benefit from a dose of blood-meal bone-meal mix. This should be mixed into the lower soil immediately before the seed potatoes are planted. Potatoes can also be grown in compost. Compost tea or homemade fertilizer can also be used.

How to transplant: Do not transplant.

When to harvest: New potatoes are harvested four to six weeks after the potatoes have sprouted above the soil or straw. Note that new potatoes are often the size of a quarter, and sometimes a bit larger. Mature potatoes are harvested when the potato plant has died back completely.

How to preserve: When harvesting your potatoes, be certain that you do not cut or damage the skin or flesh of the potato. The most common mistake when harvesting is using a shovel or garden fork too close to the plant, which can cut the tuber. Damaged tubers are not likely to store well and should be used within a day or two. Instead, insert a garden fork on the side of the plant, deeply, and lift the whole mass of potatoes gently upward. Do not wash, clean, rub, or wipe the potatoes. Potatoes store best when touched as little as possible after harvest. Set potatoes outside, out of direct sunlight and in a dry place, for two days to harden them off. Then store the potatoes in a burlap or fabric sack, or other container with significant air flow. Potatoes must be stored in a cool, dry, dark place.

Watermelon Radish

Radishes

Rhaphanus sativus | Annual

The one thing you need to know to grow great radishes is that they love cool weather. Radishes are among the fastest growing of all bulb vegetables and are harvested early.

When to plant: Plant as soon as soil can be worked in spring. A succession planting can be done each week through spring.

Where to plant: In clay or loam.

How to plant: Plant the seeds a quarter-inch deep in moist soil.

How to fertilize: Not necessary.

How to transplant: Radishes do not like to be transplanted.

When to harvest: Harvest as soon as the bulbs appear. The longer radishes stay in the ground, the hotter their flavor and the more woody their texture.

How to preserve: Radishes can be pickled.

RECOMMENDED VARIETIES

- 'Watermelon' is a variety of radish that is a little sweeter than most radishes and has a green/white outer color and a red inner color resembling a watermelon.
- Cincinnati Market: In light soil, these produce long, straight roots that can be used in cooking like carrots. These are red on the top of the root and white on the bottom.

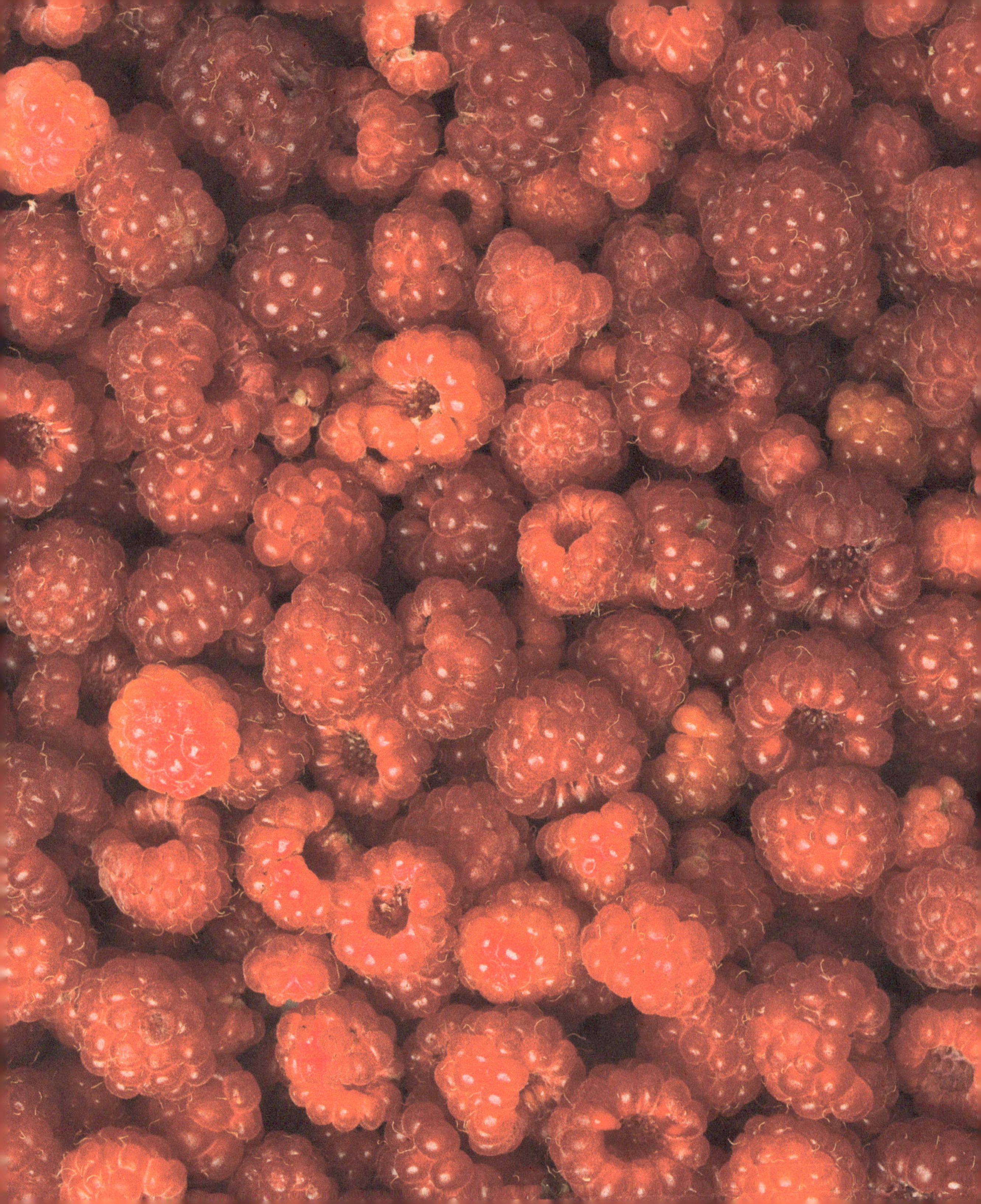

Raspberries

Perennial

Because I am perhaps the world's biggest lover of raspberries, this book—which I intended to be just about vegetables—does not feel complete without information about my favorite garden feast. We grow a lot of raspberries, and rarely do any of them make it into the house to be made into something. Instead, we have a sometimes-unfriendly competition. On any summer day, we get up and go eat raspberries straight off the bushes for breakfast. Or brunch or lunch or dinner or a snack. The rule is simple: Whoever gets to them first gets them. If you go out to the raspberry patch and find that all the ripe ones have been devoured, you better be the early bird next time. Perhaps the truest sign of love in our family is when someone brings you a handful of ripe raspberries. We grow gold raspberries, and we grow red raspberries in both June-bearing and ever-bearing types (more on this in a moment). I've given more than one hundred raspberry plants away over the years, because raspberries will slowly spread. My favorite raspberry recipe of all time is Raspberry Valentine Pie, which can be found in my cookbook *The Stevia Solution*.

When to plant: Once. Because raspberries are a perennial plant, you should plant them wherever you want them to grow for years. They will slowly spread. When you have plants that you don't need, it isn't hard to give them away to family, friends, and neighbors. If you want plants, it's usually easy to get them for free on social media or sites like your local Freecycle.org group.

Where to plant: Raspberries tolerate a wide range of soils, but the big concern is that you don't want them infested with weeds. Planting them in a shallow raised bed is best if you want to harvest for years without a lot of weeding. Because raspberries are surprisingly shallow rooted bushes, you can line the bed with weed barrier before you fill it to ensure there are no weeds. Leave a small hole in the center of the weed barrier (the size of your hand) to give access for worms, which increase natural soil health.

How to plant: Raspberries are widely sold as live plants. Place them in a prepared hole and water them well, keeping the soil level in the pot at the soil level in your garden. I will mention here that if a plant produces true progeny, I do not consider it to be a hybrid even if the plant was hybridized by human intervention. This is an important distinction to me because hybrid raspberry bushes are not self-suiciding like most hybrid seeds, and I can give away the extra plants or even sell them in most cases. So even though some raspberry varieties are technically hybrid plants, in this instance it does not matter.

How to fertilize: Raspberries produce larger berries if they are given a dose of compost tea or homemade fertilizer when the bush begins to produce flowers.

How to prune: Raspberries can be pruned in late autumn or early spring each year by cutting the bushes uniformly to be about twenty-four inches tall. This will help produce slightly larger berries, if that is something that you worry about. At our house, sometimes we get around to pruning them, and at least half the time, if not more, we don't, and they always produce great berries. So whether you want to spend the time to prune them is up to you. If it has been several years, your bushes will probably benefit from a pruning.

When to harvest: Raspberries are fully sweet when they are soft to the touch and easily slip off the bush when gently pulled. If you are worried that birds will beat you to them, plant more bushes, or plant the yellow raspberry types, which birds don't bother for whatever reason. Some raspberry types are "June-bearing," meaning that they produce a flush of berries in that month and then are done. Others are "ever-bearing," meaning that instead of bearing a lot of fruit in one month, they produce smaller amounts of berries but do so all season. June-bearing are preferred for people who want to freeze or make jam from their berries. Ever-bearing are preferred for fresh eating as long as possible. My suggestion is to grow both kinds.

RECOMMENDED VARIETIES

Any variety is a good variety, but don't limit yourself to just the red types. Plants with thorns are sweeter and more flavorful than thornless types. I always grow the berries with thorns, and have never found the thorns to be a real problem because the plants are not dense.

Rutabaga

(Swedes or Swede Turnips)

Brassica napus | Biennial

When to plant: Rutabaga prefer a cool growing season. If your growing season is not cool, plant in a greenhouse in earliest spring, or plant outside in late summer for autumn harvesting.

Where to plant: Rutabaga will tolerate a wide range of soils but prefer loam.

How to plant: Plant seeds a half-inch deep and eight inches apart. Keep moist to germination, which can take two weeks or more in cool soil.

How to fertilize: Rutabaga benefits from a dose of compost tea or homemade fertilizer when young and once again when the bulb begins to develop.

How to transplant: Do not transplant.

When to harvest: Bulbs can be harvested at any size.

How to preserve: Carefully lift the bulb from the soil. Trim the leaves and stems from the top without cutting into the bulb. Do not wash, wipe, clean, or rub the bulb. "Plant" the bulb in damp sand or pine shavings for winter storage and keep in a cool, dark, dry place. When kept in this way, rutabaga will keep for months.

RECOMMENDED VARIETIES

Any heirloom variety

Spinach

Spinacia oleracea | Annual and Semi-Biennial

When to plant: Spinach is planted in spring, or it's planted in late summer or early autumn for fall harvesting. It's tolerant of cold and can be planted in winter in a greenhouse or under a cold frame, cloche, row cover, or other protection. America Spinach is the best variety for cold-soil growing.

Where to plant: Spinach tolerates a wide range of soils but does best in loam or compost-amended soil.

How to plant: Plant seeds a quarter-inch deep and six inches apart. Keep moist to germination.

How to fertilize: Spinach doesn't need fertilizer in healthy soil. If your soil is poor, amend with compost or apply compost tea or homemade fertilizer once or twice.

How to transplant: Spinach is usually seeded directly in the garden but can be started indoors and transplanted if desired. There will be some "transplant shock," which will stunt the growth of the plant for two to three weeks before it reestablishes its roots.

When to harvest: Spinach leaves can be harvested at any size but have the best flavor when young.

How to preserve: Spinach can be blanched and frozen but is not generally preserved.

RECOMMENDED VARIETIES

- America Spinach is the best because it is prolific, easy to grow, and has the best cold-soil and winter tolerance. This spinach loves cold weather!

Squash and Pumpkins

Annual

Cucurbita maxima includes banana squash varieties, buttercup squash varieties, hubbard squash varieties, turban squash varieties, marrow squash varieties, as well as Amish pie, Australian pumpkin, and others.

Cucurbita mixta includes most varieties of cushaw squashes and all varieties of wild seroria squash and silver-seeded gourds, as well as Big White Crookneck, Cochita Pueblo squash, and others.

Cucurbita moschata includes most varieties of butternut squashes and cheese squashes, as well as golden cushaw, orange cushaw, orange-striped cushaw, sweet potato squash, Citrouille d'Eysines, field pumpkins, Futtsu squashes, Kikuza, Landreth, Long Island, Tennessee squashes, Napoli squashes, Rampicante (also called tromboncino), and others.

Cucurbita pepo includes most varieties of summer squashes, acorn squashes, cocozelle squashes, crookneck squashes, scallop squashes, zucchini squashes, and vegetable marrow squashes, and most gourds, as well as Connecticut field pumpkin, delicata, early prolific straightneck, Forkhook, scallopini squashes, Jack-O'-Lantern, Howden squashes, Japanese pie, Lakota, Naked Seeded, New England pie, Patisson squashes, potimarron, Rocky Mountain pie, Rondo de Nice, Straightneck, small sugar squashes, Thelma Sanders, spaghetti squash (also called vegetable spaghetti), winter pie, Xochitlan Pueblo, and others.

When to plant: All squash species are best directly seeded in the garden after all danger of frost has passed.

Where to plant: Squash tolerates a wide range of soils but prefer loam.

How to plant: Plant seeds one inch deep. Keep moist to germination, which takes about a week.

How to fertilize: If you have healthy soil, squash should not be fertilized. Summer squash in particular should not be fertilized because this will only encourage the fruits to rapidly grow past their best size and flavor. Pumpkins and winter squash generally don't need fertilizer, but if your soil is poor, you can apply a dose of compost tea or homemade fertilizer when the squash bulbs begin to form.

How to transplant: Squashes prefer not to be transplanted but can be started indoors if necessary. However, because transplant shock delays growth for two to three weeks while the plant establishes new hair roots (tiny, critical roots), if you have a short growing season like I do, it is best to direct-seed short-season (short day-count) varieties instead of transplanting. All varieties sold at SeedRenaissance.com are the shortest day-count varieties available.

When to harvest: Harvest squash after the leaves of the plant have died around the squash.

How to preserve: Specific varieties of squash are grown for winter storage in a dry, cool, dark place.

RECOMMENDED VARIETIES

- **Atlantic Giant Pumpkins:** Okay, here's a confession about why I love these so much—in a short growing season, or if I am late planting, these pumpkins grow so fast that I still get great pumpkins, even if they are not giant! If you have a full summer season, these can grow huge!

- **Connecticut Field Pumpkin:** The old, gold standard. This is the traditional Halloween pumpkin. And it stores through the whole winter.

- **Early Prolific Straight-Neck Summer Squash:** Vintage winner! This beautiful, bright-yellow squash won All-American Selection in 1938. It is tender and straight—tastes like summer!

- **Early Yellow Crookneck Squash:** Long a summer favorite, this is the yellow bumpy squash that everyone loves. Matures quickly and produces well. About twenty seeds per pack.

- **Potimarron Winter Squash:** Teardrop shaped, dense, intensely red winter squash with fantastic storage. These are on the small side, but they are almost solid with flesh inside—worth growing just for the flavor, but also because these squash are prolific!

- **Rampicante Italian Vining Zucchini:** Everyone should grow this! It is sweeter than all other zucchini. It is a summer squash in summer, but if you leave it on the vine, it changes color and texture to become a winter squash with a butternut texture and flavor. It's a treasure I am never without in my garden!

- **Squash Waltham Butternut:** Traditional butternut squash that so many people like to bake in winter. You can also use this for ravioli filling.

- **Zucchini Costata Romanesco:** This beautiful old Italian is a staple of the garden. A slightly ribbed zucchini with a great flavor.

Strawberries

Perennial

When to plant: Once. Because strawberries are a perennial plant, you should plant them wherever you want them to grow for years. Many varieties of red strawberries will produce vines and spread out, so you may want to "confine" your strawberries in a frame or bed.

Where to plant: Strawberries tolerate a wide range of soils, but the big concern is that you don't want them infested with weeds. Planting them in a raised bed is best if you want to harvest for years without a lot of weeding. Because strawberries are shallow-rooted plants, you can line the bed with weed barrier before you fill it to ensure there are no weeds. Leave a small hole in the center of the weed barrier about the size of your hand to give access for worms, which increase natural soil health.

How to plant: Strawberries can be started from true seed. Seeds are typically started indoors and moved outdoors in spring when the plants are roughly an inch tall. Strawberries are also widely sold as live plants, which will produce runners (vines with new plants) over time. As with raspberries, if a plant produces true progeny, I do not consider it to be a hybrid, even if the plant was hybridized by human intervention. This is an important distinction to me because strawberry plants are not self suiciding like most hybrid seeds, and I can give away the extra plants or even sell them in most cases, so even though most red strawberries are technically hybrid plants, in this instance it does not matter.

How to fertilize: Strawberries produce larger berries if they are given a dose of compost tea or homemade fertilizer when the plant begins to produce flowers.

How to transplant: Let the new plants at the end of the strawberry runner vines root themselves firmly to the ground. Cut the vine and dig up the plant without removing the soil from the roots. Move the plants to the desired location, press them firmly into a prepared hole, and water generously.

When to harvest: Strawberries are fully sweet before they are fully red (if you are growing red strawberry varieties). If you are worried that the birds will beat you to the strawberries, you can pick them when they are mostly red instead of all the way ripe. Some strawberry types are "June-bearing," meaning that they produce a flush of fruit in that month and then are done. Others are "everbearing," meaning that instead of bearing a lot of fruit in one month, they produce smaller amounts of fruit but do so all season. June-bearing are preferred for people who want to freeze or can strawberries. Ever-bearing are preferred for fresh eating as long as possible. My suggestion is to grow both kinds.

RECOMMENDED VARIETIES

Any variety is a good variety, but don't limit yourself to just the red types. Look for seasonal offerings of live plants of pineapple-flavored white strawberries. We also sell Alpine strawberry seeds and other varieties as available.

Sunflowers

Helianthus annuus | Annual

When to plant: Plant sunflowers direct-seeded in the garden after all danger of frost has passed.

Where to plant: Sunflowers will tolerate a wide range of soils, including clay and sand.

How to plant: Plant seeds one inch deep and twelve inches apart for medium-flower producers, or eighteen inches apart or more for sunflower varieties that produce giant heads.

How to fertilize: Sunflowers may be fertilized with compost tea or homemade fertilizer once when young and a second time when the flower head begins to form.

How to transplant: Sunflowers are generally not transplanted.

When to harvest: Harvest the flower head after it has dried naturally in the garden.

How to preserve: Birds will likely begin harvesting your sunflower seeds before they are fully dried. To prevent this, you may want to wrap your flower heads in breathable cotton fabric. Dried heads can be stored in a cool, dry, dark place in a sealed container where they are safe from mice, or the seeds can be rubbed from the flower head using your hands, covered with leather gloves. If the seeds are not fully dry, allow them to air dry on a cookie sheet. When they are fully dry, you can store the seeds in a sealed container. To separate the seeds from the hulls, the method I have found to work best is to run the seeds through a grain mill on the most open setting. I have both electric and hand-crank flour grinders, and they generally have settings from coarse to fine. Run the seeds through the most coarse setting allowed by your machine. This will crack the seeds open without grinding them on most machines. You may need to run them through the machine a couple of times to crack all the seeds open, or adjust your coarseness setting upward slightly, depending on the size of your seeds. You can then use a sieve to separate the seeds from the hulls.

RECOMMENDED VARIETIES

Any heirloom variety

Sweet Potatoes

Ipomoea batatas | Annual

B*uying slips:* I recommend ordering slips from Sand Hill Preservation Center at SandHillPreservation.com. I suggest you order in January or February because the most in-demand varieties sell out extremely fast. If there is a company offering a larger selection than Sand Hill, I don't know about it. If you have a short growing season, choose varieties that mature in ninety days or less.

Note on voles: The biggest problem I have had growing "sweets" in my ninety-two-day growing season is not not getting usable roots (I do) but getting to the roots before the voles. Voles are often mistaken for mice. They love my garden because, well, I'm lovable, I guess. They live in shallow tunnels under any rocks or wood they can find. As long as food is plentiful, they are not usually too much of a problem, but at the first sign of cold, they start voraciously eating everything they can find—just about the time when the sweet potatoes are ready to harvest. I have to keep a close eye on them, and I have learned the hard way that voles love sweet potatoes, so I should not delay in harvesting them. It is better to harvest smaller roots than no roots at all!

When to plant: June or July. Sweet potatoes, like tomato plants, basically do no growing until the weather is warm.

Where to plant: Sweet potatoes, like common potatoes, prefer loamy, friable soil that is rich in organic matter.

How to fertilize: The soil you plant your slips in should have some compost mixed in it. Otherwise, sweet potatoes don't need fertilizer. Fertilizing them too much can result in huge roots, which don't store well for winter eating. Give your sweet potatoes one dose of compost tea, made in warm water, in midsummer, if you desire.

How to preserve: Sweet potatoes bruise easily and must be treated with care.

Remember that unlike many common potatoes, sweet potatoes grow shallowly. Dig them up gently and carefully using your gloved hands and a garden fork. Do not wash! Sweet potatoes, like all garden root vegetables, should not be washed for storage. Leave your sweet potatoes outside for a week in a place where they can get at least some sun but are not exposed to rain. This lets them "harden" and "cure" for storage. After a week, store them in a burlap or mesh bag like potatoes. Set them in the bag gently—sweet potatoes bruise even more easily than common potatoes. Sweet potatoes with any damage should be used first and not stored with the others, because a rotting sweet potato can spoil the others around it. Store in low humidity in a cool, dry, dark place.

RECOMMENDED VARIETIES

In the Sand Hill catalog, you will find different colors—white, purple, orange, yellow, pink, and red. Some produce huge vines more than a dozen feet long. Some grow just on a small bush. Choose the varieties that suit your space and curiosity.

Swiss Chard

(Chard)

Beta vulgaris | Biennial

When to plant: Plant in mid-spring or early autumn.

Where to plant: Swiss chard tolerates a wide variety of soil types, including clay and sand.

How to plant: Plant a quarter-inch deep and keep moist to germination, which may take two weeks, or longer if the soil is cold.

How to fertilize: Swiss chard does not need fertilizer.

How to transplant: Swiss chard can be started indoors and transplanted outside in mid-spring, but because of the temperature shock, there is little to be gained by transplanting, and it is not normally done.

When to harvest: Swiss chard leaves can be harvested at any size.

How to preserve: Swiss chard is not preserved.

RECOMMENDED VARIETIES

- Bright Lights Swiss chard has yellow, red, purple, and green stems and tastes good too. Bright Lights can change color depending on temperature and is most often red when grown in winter in my geothermal greenhouse. Bright Lights easily self-seeds in a no-till garden, and if you plant it once and allow some plants to go to seed, you will likely have Swiss chard growing in your garden for the rest of your life.

Tomatoes

Solanum lycopersicum | Annual

When to plant: Tomatoes can be planted indoors eight weeks before your last frost date.

Where to plant: Tomatoes prefer loamy soil but will tolerate a wide range of soils.

How to plant: Lightly rake the seed into the soil and keep moist until germination, which will take a few days in warm soil.

How to fertilize: Tomatoes benefit from soil that is heavily amended with compost, as well as crushed household eggshells for extra calcium and a few old nails for iron. Tomatoes also do well with compost tea applications once every month or blood-meal and bone-meal that is mixed into the soil when the plants are transplanted outdoors.

How to transplant: Believe it or not, small tomato plants transplant best. No matter how hard you work to start your tomatoes early, they will suffer from transplant shock when you move them from indoors to outdoors. Tomatoes that are started indoors must be kept in full sunlight or they will quickly get leggy and weak. The larger the tomato plant is, the greater its temperature shock will be when transplanted. In my garden, my greenhouse transplants produce tomatoes later each year than my Snow Fairy tomatoes that self-seed in the open garden!

When to harvest: Tomatoes are ripe when you press them with your finger and the flesh springs back.

How to preserve fresh: There are varieties of tomatoes called "Longkeeper" and "Winter Grape" (among others) that have been bred for years to be harvested as green tomatoes at the end of the growing season and then brought into the cellar or any dark, cold, dry place where they will slowly ripen. For best results, put each green tomato into a clean egg cup in a cardboard egg box. Leave the boxes open when storing. Check the tomatoes weekly and use them as they turn red in the dark. If a tomato turns soft, throw it out. Save the seeds from your longest-keeping tomatoes to use in your garden the next year.

RECOMMENDED VARIETIES

I have probably tested six hundred varieties of heirloom tomatoes, and I test about fifty more each year. Out of all of these, here are the varieties I recommend:

- **Stupice:** This is an old Siberian variety, which is the earliest to ever produce tomatoes in my garden. These are determinate, meaning they set fruit in a short period of time, which makes them great for harvesting for canning or freezing.

- **Clackamas Blueberry:** This is a rare variety bred in Oregon. It is truly blue and is amazing. The flavor is wonderful. They are very early, but don't harvest them until the blue tomatoes turn red on the bottom and are soft to the touch. Clackamas Blueberry is unusual not only for its color but also because it is one of the rare short-season varieties that ripens tomatoes over a long, indeterminate window of time. People go crazy for the unusual color and great flavor! Seeds sell out quickly each year.

- **German Queen:** A visitor who came to tour my garden handed me the first German Queen I had ever seen, and wow, what a tomato it is! These ripen just before the first frost in my garden, but they are huge. Every single tomato is over a pound, and some are over two pounds! They are great slicers, and we use them extensively for making and freezing sauce.

- **Roma:** This is an old favorite, developed in Italy and used as a favorite saucing tomato for centuries. Why? Because this variety is low on seeds and juice and heavy on thick, delicious flesh that make a wonderful rich tomato sauce.

- **Amish Paste:** Like Roma, these are huge, fleshy saucing tomatoes that are also low on seeds and juice with thick flesh and perfect flavor for sauce or sandwiches.

- **Snow Fairy:** This Siberian variety is the best for greenhouse and winter production of tomatoes. Probably no one in the world has tested as many winter tomato varieties as I have, and this one is hands-down the winner!

Turnips

Brassica rapa | Biennial

When to plant: Anytime after the ground can be worked in spring. The earlier you plant them, the longer they will take to germinate.

Where to plant: Turnips happily tolerate a wide variety of soils.

How to plant: Lightly rake the seed into the soil. If planting rows, plant six inches apart. Keep moist to germination.

How to fertilize: Turnips don't need fertilizer. Fertilizing them only encourages them to outgrow their best size for flavor and storage.

How to transplant: Turnips are not generally transplanted but are planted directly in the garden.

When to harvest: Harvest the bulbs at any usable size. The leaves can also be harvested for eating at any size but taste best when young.

How to preserve: Dig the turnips without damaging them. Trim the leaves, leaving up to an inch of stems. Do not cut the root. Do not wash. Store in a cool, dry, dark place in damp sand or damp sawdust.

RECOMMENDED VARIETIES

- **Purple Top White Globe Turnip:** This turnip has wonderful heirloom turnip taste, is a hardy plant, and is great for using in roast vegetable dishes and soups. It has a beautiful purple top around a white globe, with white flesh inside. Purple top white globe is an excellent self-seeder as long as you keep it isolated from other *Brassica rapa* varieties. It does great in winter greenhouses!

Watermelon

Citrullus lanatus | Annual

When to plant: Plant after all danger of frost has passed.

Where to plant: Watermelons tolerate a wide range of soils, including sand and clay. What watermelons want most is warm soil. Historically, watermelons were planted in rows of manure mixed with soil so that the natural composting action of the manure would warm the roots and the plants would thrive and also be well fertilized. Today, many gardeners grow watermelons in black plastic to warm the soil. If you are using plastic, lay a row of plastic and weight it down with rocks. Cut small holes in the center of the plastic, about five feet apart. Plant the seeds in the holes. Keep soil moist to germination.

How to plant: Plant seeds a half-inch deep directly in garden soil.

How to fertilize: Use compost tea or homemade fertilizer twice: once when the plant is young and a second time when the first melons begin to grow.

How to transplant: Watermelons can be started indoors and transplanted, but truth be told, there is not much point. Whenever a plant is moved from perfect indoor conditions to the outdoors, the plant undergoes a condition called transplant shock. The roots are disturbed, and the tiny, almost invisible "hair roots" that the plant depends on are damaged. The sun burns the tender leaves, which have never been exposed to direct sunlight before. The wind also burns the leaves. It can take the plant several weeks to establish itself and adjust to its new living conditions. Meanwhile, watermelon plants that came up after being directly seeded in the garden do not suffer transplant shock, because they were never indoors. Transplanted watermelons usually bear fruit no earlier than direct-seeded plants, and often transplants are slower to produce fruit because they must spend so much time adjusting to the shock.

When to harvest: Unlike peaches and some other fruits, watermelons do not ripen after they are picked, so if you pick an unripe watermelon, it will never finish ripening. Here is how to determine whether a watermelon is ripe. Watermelons grow on vines. On the vines will be curly tendrils. When the tendril nearest to the watermelon—and on the same vine as the watermelon—is dry and dead, the watermelon is ripe. Please note that the vine will not be dead and dry, just the tendril that is both on the same vine as the melon and nearest the melon on that vine.

How to preserve: Some watermelon varieties are "keepers," meaning they can store in a cool, dark, dry place for weeks or even months and still be delicious when cut open. These are sometimes called "Christmas watermelons" or "winter watermelons." Look for specific varieties with this trait. Otherwise, watermelons should be eaten soon after they are picked.

RECOMMENDED VARIETIES

I'm going to give two answers in this section. My first answer is this: I'd recommend any heirloom variety with a day count that fits in your growing season. Where I live, this means I can grow only the fastest-maturing watermelon varieties, which I'll list in a moment. My second answer is either self-reliant or just plain stupid, depending on who you ask, and a lot of people vote "stupid." I don't like plastic in my garden. People have tried to argue with me on this, tried to convince me how futile and ridiculous I'm being, but it doesn't change the fact that I don't like plastic in my garden.

"But you are being at least dumb, if not hypocritical," people say to me. "You have hoses in your garden. Those are plastic. You have cold frames in your garden. Some of those use plastic. The underground pipes that bring the water through your yard are plastic. There is some plastic weed fabric on your paths. There is plastic in your garden, so who cares if you use black plastic to warm the soil for your melons?"

And these people are right. I bow to their logic. But I still can't get onboard. Here's why: using plastic to grow melons produces melons that depend on plastic to be grown, if that makes any sense. When my grandfather was a boy, he grew huge melons, and he never used plastic. He couldn't remember what variety those melon seeds were, unfortunately, but in all likelihood, the variety is now extinct. Born in 1921, Phill Nielson was growing melons in the Great Basin desert (where I still live today) from boyhood until World War II broke out. They did not use plastic, and the melons he grew then were larger than any modern melons and tasted better, he told me. In my whole life, I have never met anyone in my growing area who could grow large melons without black plastic. I'm convinced that our watermelon varieties, once ideally suited for our climate, have either gone extinct totally or have been genetically weakened because they are grown using pseudo-climates like black plastic. So I refuse to get on board. Will the

zombie apocalypse one day make it impossible to get black plastic, rending everyone's watermelon raising useless? Probably not. Probably people will happily be using black plastic in their gardens for the rest of time. So I'm alone here, but I hate weakening our seeds, and I do not like the way black plastic looks in my garden—like I'm dependent on plastic to grow food. And I probably am. Who among us can live a plastic-free life today? No one I've ever met. But I am going to go on raising melons without plastic—or trying to, at least. Your melons will be much happier and more productive with black plastic, so you should probably let me be alone on this crusade. With all that said, keep in mind that I have tested every single "early" heirloom watermelon variety on earth—every single one. These are what I recommend:

- **White Sugar Lump:** This is an exceedingly rare watermelon variety. This variety is hugely important because it is, by far, the best variety I have ever found for growing without plastic. It is prolific with no plastic. Unfortunately, I am not joking when I say the seeds are almost extinct. Where I live, it is impossible to grow out "true" watermelon seed that is not cross-pollinated by neighbors' watermelon plants, so I have not yet been able to "save" this variety, but I do have some seeds. I have found a reliable volunteer with a huge, remote property who has agreed to grow out a crop of these seed for me, so I hope that for the time being, I can at least offer these seeds for sale again. Watermelons are not easy to hand-pollinate and keep pure, so for the moment, I am still working on saving these seeds the old-fashioned way—by growing them in isolation. This old variety (1) tastes great, (2) ripens early, and (3) grows well without black plastic. This is a so-called "icebox" melon, meaning that when it is mature, it is about the size of your head. This is also a great melon because the flesh inside is entirely white but tastes just like red watermelon.

Planting Chart

START IN THE GREENHOUSE	basil, celery (if planting indoors), rutabaga
START INDOORS	broccoli (three months before you intend to move plants outside), Brussels sprouts (two to three months prior to last expected frost), cabbage (plant in full sun or under artificial light), eggplant (six weeks prior to last expected frost), tomatoes (eight weeks prior to last expected frost)
SOW SEED DIRECTLY AS SOON AS SOIL CAN BE WORKED IN THE SPRING	Asian greens, beets, cabbage, cauliflower (plant in mid-spring and use cold frame to protect), carrots, sunchokes, leeks, lettuce, mustard greens, onion seed, orach, parsnips, peas, radishes, turnips

PLANT IN SPRING	asparagus (as seeds, crowns, or root cuttings), Chinese cabbage, collards, kale, onion bulbs, potatoes (in straw beds), raspberries, strawberries, Swiss chard
AFTER ALL THREAT OF FROST HAS PASSED	basil, cantaloupe, beans, corn, cucumber, edamame, lettuce, mustard greens, peppers, potatoes (in compost beds), spinach, squash, pumpkins, sunflowers, Swiss chard, watermelon
MID-SUMMER	celery (outdoors), sweet potatoes
LATE SUMMER OR EARLY AUTUMN	Asian greens, Chinese cabbage, garlic (northern climates), lettuce, mustard greens, onion bulbs, onion seed, rutabaga, spinach

Rutabagas

Your ancestors knew how to live self-sufficiently—now you can follow in their footsteps! Bestselling author Caleb Warnock is back with a new collection of money-saving and healthy-living skills to help your family gain independence and self-reliance.

Learn how to

- grow self-seeding vegetables
- build raised garden beds using step-by-step instructions
- collect water from rain and snow
- make your own laundry detergent
- rind wild vegetables for everyday eating

Whether you're growing an organic family garden or running a no-nonsense household, *More Forgotten Skills of Self-Sufficiency* is a must-have guide to becoming truly self- reliant for you and your family.

Many people dream of becoming self-reliant during times of fluctuating prices and uncertain job security. Using truly simple techniques, you can cultivate the pioneers' independence to provide safety against lost wages, harsh weather, economic recession, and commercial food contamination and shortages. Now you can discover the lost survival skills they knew, used, and passed down for genera- tions—skills such as how to

- grow hardy, perennial, and long-keeping vegetables
- revive the pioneer seed bank Bake with pioneer yeast
- create a straw cellar
- cook with forgotten recipes
- and more!

Hallie doesn't belong in Tippy Canoe, Montana. She's a California girl used to sunshine and warmth—not cold and snow. But after the unexpected death of her estranged husband, she braves the winter weather to wrap up some of his estate details, only to discover that she doesn't fit in, and none of the townspeople like her.

That is, except for the town's handsome mayor, who takes quite an interest in Hallie.

But when his life starts to spiral out of control, she must decide if he's worth sticking around for in the long term. Join Hallie in this fast-paced, hilarious romance as she learns that sometimes love is the only remedy for a broken heart.

This is the book you've been waiting for! With groundbreaking information about the health benefits of natural yeast, this book will revolutionize the way you bake! Improve your digestive health and happiness with these delicious recipes you can't find anywhere else!

Be sure to try the

- blueberry cream muffins
- quick and easy crepes
- garlic rosemary sourdough
- whimsy rolls
- no-knead bread

From quick and easy treats for a busy day to elaborate creations for special events, you'll find something tasty and nutritious to tempt everyone's taste buds!

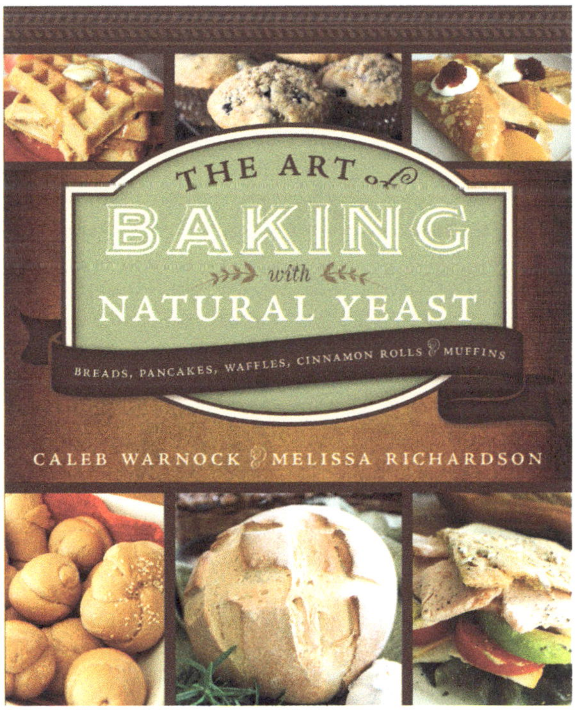

Misconceptions about winter gardening are everywhere: it's too difficult, slow, or even impossible. Feeding your family fresh food from your own backyard garden all winter long is far easier and less time-consuming than you might imagine. In *Backyard Winter Gardening*, you'll learn

- how to grow winter produce without electricity, artificial heating, or lighting
- how cold temperatures don't have to result in a dead garden
- how to build a cold frame, a hotbed, and even a geothermal greenhouse for protection from harsh weather
- how children will love vegetables if they take part in the gardening
- how winter gardening protects against economic turmoil, teaches self-providence, and protects your food from unknown chemicals and contamination

This latest volume in Caleb Warnock's popular Forgotten Skills series teaches you how to grow, harvest, and store your own herbs. Learn how to use them in natural remedies for safe, reliable healing, even when you can't get to a doctor.

Inside you'll find

- tips on how to use specific herbs to treat problems like infections, nausea, acne, and the common cold
- step-by-step recipes for healing tinctures, medicinal teas, and homemade vinegars
- in-depth guides to common herbs, where to find them, when to pick them, what part of the plant to use, and how to prepare your compounds
- information about how to avoid common and dangerous mistakes and how to become a responsible herb collector

This invaluable book will keep your whole family healthy for years to come!

Savor the taste of sumptuous meals made from 100 percent natural whole foods—many you can grow yourself. This DIY cookbook helps you make the most from the healthy, wholesome ingredients you want to feed your family. With delicious recipes to eat tonight, plus lots more you can make ahead and store, this is a comprehensive resource for experienced chefs and amateur cooks alike.

Easy and irresistibly yummy, these recipes make healthy eating fun and budget-friendly. And with such a wide variety of meals to choose from, you'll find something to please every palate.

Imagine gourmet chocolates and confections—all made in your own kitchen! Don't waste your money on store-bought treats. With *Hand-Dipped*, learn to create decadent homemade sweets like

- cherry cordials
- salted caramel chocolate truffles
- peanut brittle
- luxe chocolate fondue

Armed with tips on melting, dipping, and molding, as well as dozens of rich recipes, you'll be sure to satisfy any sweet tooth. Indulge your taste buds with luxurious, easy recipes from *Hand-Dipped*!

About the Author

Caleb Warnock is the owner SeedRenaissance.com, where he sells only heirloom seed varieties that he has evaluated in an organic garden for performance in earliness, flavor, production, storage, cold-soil tolerance, winter harvest ability, and self-seeding capacity, without petrochemical fertilizer, pesticides, or herbicides. If he doesn't love a variety, he doesn't sell it. Every seed is guaranteed pure—*never* hybrid, GMO, patented, or corporate owned. "Our food supply *must* remain in the public domain," Caleb says. "Join me in creating a renaissance in our backyard gardens."

Caleb was raised in the kitchens and gardens of the last generation to provide family meals without relying on the grocery store. He has won more than a dozen awards for journalism and literature, and he regularly teaches "Forgotten Skills" classes on topics ranging from winter greenhouse construction, cheese making, cold frame gardening, and more. To reach the author, visit CalebWarnock.blogspot.com or email calebwarnock@yahoo.com.

0 26575 13415 5